Guide to
Cambridge Architecture
Ten Walking Tours

The MIT Press
Cambridge, Massachusetts,
and London, England

Guide to
Cambridge Architecture
Ten Walking Tours

Robert Bell Rettig

Cambridge Historical Commission
Albert B. Wolfe, Chairman
Henry D. Winslow, Vice Chairman
Dwight H. Andrews
Arthur H. Brooks, Jr.
Rosamond Howe
Hugh M. Lyons
Robert Grant Neiley

Alternates
James F. Clapp, Jr.
Charles W. Eliot, 2d
James C. Hopkins, Jr.

Cambridge City Council
Walter J. Sullivan, Mayor
Barbara Ackermann
Edward A. Crane
Thomas W. Danehy
Bernard Goldberg
Daniel J. Hayes, Jr.
Thomas H. D. Mahoney
Alfred E. Vellucci
Cornelia B. Wheeler

City Manager
James L. Sullivan

Published by arrangement with the
Cambridge Historical Commission,
City Hall Annex, 57 Inman Street,
Cambridge, Massachusetts 02139

For illustration credits see page following
tour O.

Set in "Monophoto" Univers
Printed and bound in the United States of
America by Halliday Lithograph Corporation
Library of Congress catalog card number:
69–14407

Guide to
Cambridge Architecture
Ten Walking Tours

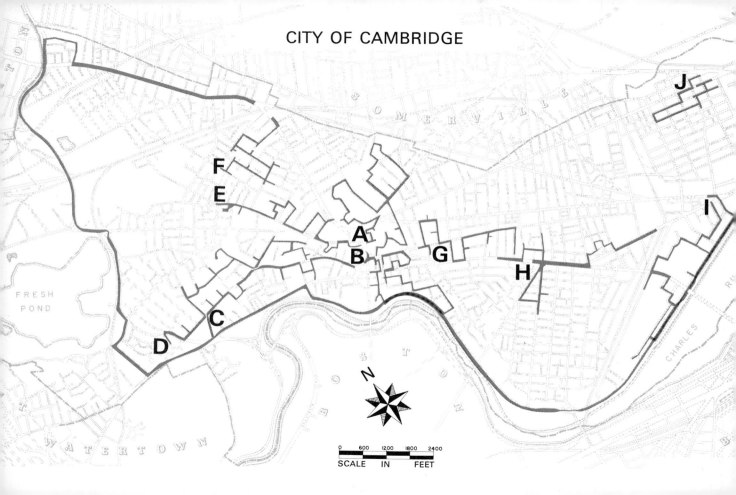

CITY OF CAMBRIDGE

SOMERVILLE

J

F

E

A

B

I

G

H

FRESH
POND

C

D

BOSTON

CHARLES RIVER

WATERTOWN

N

SCALE IN FEET

0   600   1200   1800   2400

Introduction

This book is intended as a field guide to the architecture of Cambridge, Massachusetts. Organized into ten walking tours, it presents Cambridge buildings just as they are—varied in age and quality, often haphazardly related, yet interesting enough to warrant careful study.

For a city of fewer than 100,000 people, Cambridge is rich in the quality and variety of its architecture. Buildings of all types, styles, and periods are represented, from the early 18th century to the present. Because of this wealth, the City of Cambridge, through its Historical Commission, has undertaken a comprehensive survey of the city's architecture, a survey unique in scope among American cities. This guidebook is one result of that survey.

Since 1964 a staff of architectural historians has been conducting a building-by-building inventory in Cambridge, supplementing its observations by extensive research in deeds, tax records, building permits, newspapers, and other sources. The survey has amassed a substantial body of information about a large number of Cambridge buildings—not only well-known or obviously important buildings but also more modest vernacular structures. Part of the survey program is the publication of illustrated reports on different parts of the city, with discussion of historical background, architectural development, and environmental character. A report on East Cambridge was published in 1965, one on Mid Cambridge in 1967, and one on Cambridgeport will appear in 1969; others will follow. At the conclusion of the survey a single-volume history of Cambridge architecture will be possible.

This guide is not such a history, nor is it a summary of or substitute for the individual survey reports. Rather, it is a kind of geographical index to the material gathered by the survey, organized so that residents and visitors may walk around Cambridge and have some readily accessible information about the buildings they see. A walking-tour format was chosen because Cambridge is densely enough settled to make walking the best way to get from one interesting building to the next. Furthermore, walking permits proper time to appreciate both the buildings and their context.

The tours in this guide (except for

"Other Points of Interest" at the end) have been planned exclusively for walking; anyone who tries to drive along the routes will be frustrated by one-way streets, dead ends, and even places where cars are expressly forbidden. Each tour is designed to be autonomous, but several of the tours connect with one another and could well be taken consecutively. The tours should be taken in the direction presented rather than in reverse, because the information in each is arranged for cumulative effect. For the convenience of users, the tours have been arranged to coordinate wherever possible with public transportation.

Harvard Square, the first settled part of Cambridge, is still the most active shopping, transportation, and tourist center. For this reason, the first two tours in this guide (Harvard Yard and North, Harvard Square and South) begin and end in Harvard Square; three others (Brattle Street, Garden Street, and Dana Hill) begin close by. The North of Brattle tour connects with the Brattle Street tour, Avon Hill with Garden Street, and Central Square with Dana Hill. The final two tours, M.I.T. and East Cambridge, begin and end at convenient MBTA stations— Kendall Square and Lechmere. Information about the various tours and the routes they follow can be found on the opening pages of each section, where tour maps are also published. Background material on Cambridge history is provided in an introductory chapter.

The size and length of this book have been restricted in order to make it useful as a field guide. Inevitably, many good buildings have had to be omitted because they made the individual tours too long or because they duplicated other buildings discussed. In certain parts of the city—particularly along the Charles River and in North Cambridge —buildings of architectural interest are too widely dispersed to produce a satisfactory walking tour. A few such buildings have therefore been included at the end as "Other Points of Interest" —the only tour that can be taken by automobile.

The tours are presented in terms of a series of entries corresponding to buildings along the route. Each entry has a small photograph and is identified by key number, building name or address, date of construction, and architect. Photographs have been kept small because they are meant for identification of buildings in the field rather than as text illustrations.

Comments under the entries point out salient features of the buildings and make reference, where called for, to history and development patterns, relationship to other buildings, and tour direction. Emphasis is on external stylistic features and environmental factors because this is the emphasis of the survey and because most Cambridge buildings are not open to the public. The sequence of entries is determined by the sequence of buildings in the environment rather than by age or importance.

Individual buildings are included in the guide for a variety of reasons — because they are architecturally or historically important, because they are typical of the district being traversed, because they come at points where the tour route changes direction, or sometimes because they are simply too large or unusual to be ignored. Inclusion in the guide does not mean that a building is among the major monuments of Cambridge architecture, although most of the city's significant structures can be found here; nor does lack of inclusion mean that a building is unimportant. The intention is to create a total picture of Cambridge architecture through direct experience with the buildings that make it up. Guide users who want more historical background, chronological discussion, and detailed analysis (particularly of plans and interiors) are referred to the Commission's series of survey reports.

Although this book is first and foremost a field guide, its potential usefulness to scholars has been considered in the provision of extensive cross-references and an index. Dates published in the guide represent — for the most part — the year construction began rather than the year of completion or occupancy. For buildings constructed after 1886, the date used is the year of issuance of a building permit; for buildings constructed before 1886, the published date is generally the year preceding the building's first appearance on city tax records. All dates (and most other facts) are documented in the files of the Cambridge Historical Commission. Even though care has been taken to check all facts for accuracy, there are bound to be errors. The Commission would appreciate having such errors brought to its attention.

An attempt has been made to keep the book as current as possible by anticipating future developments. Buildings scheduled to be demolished have generally not been included, and a few buildings not yet under construction as the guide was being prepared in 1968 have been included when it seemed likely that they would be built. Since the book is not a history of Cambridge architecture (except insofar as that history is told by the buildings that survive), demolished structures are not included and are only occasionally referred to.

The author is grateful for the stimulation of several years' dialogue with his colleagues on the Commission's survey staff—Bainbridge Bunting, Antoinette Downing, Elisabeth Mac-Dougall, Robert Nylander, and Eleanor Pearson. Their research, writings, and advice have been invaluable in the preparation of this guide and have inevitably influenced the result. He is also grateful for comments and criticism received from readers of the first draft of the guide, particularly Professor John Coolidge of Harvard, Professor Henry A. Millon of MIT, and members of the Cambridge Historical Commission. In the end, however, the author alone must be responsible for the selection and arrangement of material and for the opinions expressed herein.

R. B. R.
November 15, 1968

Summary of Cambridge History

Cambridge was founded in 1630 as a settlement of the Massachusetts Bay Colony. The idea was to create a fortified new town as the colony's seat of government, in a less vulnerable location than the exposed Boston peninsula. Although the idea came to naught (the government stayed in Boston), there were houses in Newtowne by the end of the winter of 1630–1631, and the settlement endured.

The village of Newtowne was in the vicinity of present-day Harvard Square, which has been rebuilt so many times that few traces of the 17th century survive. The early inhabitants were farmers who lived in the village and had their fields on the outskirts. To protect against marauders and to keep the cattle in, there was a palisade of willows a few hundred yards from the village center.

Newtowne was approached from Boston by one of two routes, neither very direct. One route came overland from Charlestown along the line of present-day Kirkland Street; the other route came by way of Brighton, crossing the Charles River by ferry (later bridge) near where the Larz Anderson Bridge is today. Except at this spot, there was no other river crossing to Cambridge until the end of the 18th century. The whole eastern part of town was virtually uninhabited, consisting of woods and fields, salt marshes, and tidal flats.

In 1636 the colonial government decided to establish a college, which the following year was located in Newtowne. Shortly thereafter the name of the settlement was changed to Cambridge, after the English university town. When a young minister named John Harvard died in Charlestown in 1639 and left his library and half his estate to the foundling institution, the grateful legislature named the college after him. The names of Cambridge and Harvard were thus intertwined within a decade after the initial settlement.

The earliest Harvard buildings were approximately where the center of the Old Yard is today—in the vicinity of Massachusetts and Harvard Halls (A2–3). The "college yard" was so called to distinguish it from an adjoining cow yard; the name has survived long after all the cattle have disappeared, a sole reminder of the university's humble origins. The village of

Cambridge was south and west of the college, toward the river; a portion of the 17th century street pattern still exists, although no buildings of that era survive. The Common was where it is today, except that it was larger (extending to Linnaean Street) and unenclosed. The Old Burying Ground was in its present location (E2).

The center of civic and religious affairs was a meeting house, the first one located at Dunster and Mt. Auburn Streets (site of 45 Dunster, B13). Later meeting houses faced Harvard Square, near the site of Lehman Hall (A71). The entire community formed the congregation that met in the meeting house; there were no rival churches until the founding of Christ Church (E3) in 1759. In 1829 the First Church separated into orthodox and Unitarian branches; both branches are still active, occupying 19th-century church buildings close to Harvard Square (Unitarian, E1; Congregational, E12).

Farming continued to be the principal occupation of Cambridge residents well into the 18th century, although the college also provided employment. A more important role of the college, then as now, was in providing a cultural climate that attracted to Cambridge people who might not otherwise have come. Among those who did come in the 18th century were wealthy families, notably Jamaican planters, who built substantial homes along the King's Highway to Watertown (present-day Brattle Street and Elmwood Avenue). Most of Cambridge's important mid-18th-century houses still survive—for example, the Vassall and Oliver houses (C19 and C54). Such houses, large by Cambridge standards if not by those of England, represented a wealthy, non-laboring class quite different from the ordinary run of Cambridge citizens. Animosities inevitably arose, becoming more inflamed in the years preceding the Revolution, since the families that occupied the town's large estates were nearly all Tories, loyal to the crown. Christ Church (E3) and the house of its first minister, East Apthorp (B42), were symbols of the royalist threat.

Cambridge's involvement in the Revolution came principally in the early months, when important planning decisions were made. After the Battle of Bunker Hill (June 17, 1775), initial strategy for the war was worked out in the Hastings house (long demolished) near the site of Littauer Center (A14). George Washington took command of the Continental Army in Cambridge; after a brief stay in Wadsworth House (A72), he made his headquarters in the Vassall house (C19), later the home of his Apothecary General, Andrew Craigie. Harvard dormitories (Massachusetts Hall, A2, and Hollis Hall, A5) and other Cambridge buildings (including Christ Church) served as barracks for troops; the Henry Vassall house (C17) was the first American Army medical headquarters; and the Fayerweather and Oliver houses (C50 and C54) served for brief periods as hospitals. Fortifications were constructed in the eastern part of the city; one of the most important, actively involved in the Siege of Boston, was Fort Putnam (site of Putnam School, J33). The only surviving remnant of

Cambridge's ring of Revolutionary fortifications is the modest earthworks at Fort Washington (O10), now cut off from the river.

General Washington left Cambridge in 1776, and subsequent Revolutionary War action took place elsewhere. The period after the Revolution was not a prosperous one in Cambridge, although at least one notable event occurred — the Massachusetts Constitutional Convention held in 1779 in the meeting house in Harvard Square. The document worked out there served as the model for the subsequent United States Constitution.

The year 1793 brought construction of the West Boston Bridge (site of Longfellow Bridge, O6) and the beginnings of development in the eastern part of

town, formerly just fields and marshes. Once the bridge had opened a direct connection to Boston, trade routes from the interior began to pass through Cambridge, and related mercantile activities (stores, warehouses, hostelries) grew up, particularly near the bridgehead. Work began on facilities for a deep-water port in the vicinity of Kendall Square; canals were built (a few traces of which survive), and several modest residential districts emerged near Main Street in the early years of the 19th century. The Embargo of 1807, however, brought port activities to a halt; commerce and ultimately manufacturing became dominant in that part of town. The name Cambridgeport held on, however, for the district on either side of Main Street between Kendall Square and Central Square (Tour H).

Development of East Cambridge was made possible by construction in 1807–1809 of the Canal or Craigie's Bridge (present site of the Charles River Dam). Laid out on a grid pattern of streets, the core of East Cambridge (Tour J) has maintained its residential identity down to the present, although its industrial periphery has changed over the years. The Middlesex County seat was moved to East Cambridge from Harvard Square in 1816 as a promotional venture on the part of the developers of East Cambridge; the county buildings are still there, although hardly a trace of the original Bulfinch courthouse survives (J8).

Bridge construction had an important effect on Cambridge's street pattern, for every time a new bridge was opened, one or more roads were put through from the bridgehead to established centers. Since the land in between was mostly undeveloped, the routes of these roads could be straight and direct. Cambridge Street, Hampshire Street, Broadway, Main Street, Massachusetts Avenue, Western Avenue, and River Street all originated in this way and have remained major arteries down to the present. Other streets, established as need arose or as private land was released for subdivision, related themselves to the major arteries, which quite naturally became routes for public transportation.

Because of their location and trade connections, Cambridgeport and East Cambridge were oriented more to Boston than to the village of Old Cambridge. There was considerable rivalry among the three districts, which were separated from each other by stretches of open land. East Cambridge attracted the county buildings in 1816; Cambridgeport became the seat of the town government in 1832. At one point a petition was circulated to have the eastern half of Cambridge made a separate governmental entity. In spite of such differences and rivalries, the three sections of town remained together, and Cambridge was incorporated as a city in 1846. At the time, North Cambridge was little more than a roadway to the interior of the county. The next half century brought extensive development in all parts of the city, so that by 1900 Cambridgeport, East Cambridge, and Old Cambridge had virtually merged with each other, and development had extended into North and West Cambridge as well.

Industry concentrated in the eastern part of the city because of proximity to the river and to Boston. An additional stimulus was the Grand Junction Railroad, chartered in 1852 to connect the present Boston & Maine and Boston & Albany lines. Manufacturing, staffed by increasing numbers of immigrants, engendered a need for workers' housing, which filled up much available land. Improved local transportation, such as street railways introduced in the 1850's, made Cambridge also a desirable residential suburb for people working in Boston; the college and its related intellectual community continued to attract other residents. Thus, the city was built up with all types and levels of housing, from tenements to mansions.

The pattern of 19th-century development in Cambridge was haphazard, depending on availability of land, location (particularly convenience to streetcar lines), and demand; estates were subdivided by different individuals in different ways at different times. There was no such thing as a master plan, nor was there any zoning except in the form of deed restrictions. Often, houses of varying types and sizes were built in close proximity. For example, on Dana Hill (Tour G), which developed as a residential suburb beginning in the late 1830's, large houses and modest cottages were built within sight of each other, and the occupants ranged from business and professional people to unskilled laborers. Even in the Brattle Street district (Tours C and D), where the houses and the population (largely literary and professional) were more homogeneous, there were

modest workers' houses just a block or two away toward the river.

Through most of the 19th century the Charles River remained an eyesore and a detriment to the city; it was a noxious tidal estuary bordered by marshes and mud flats. While Boston in 1856 adopted a master plan for transforming its tidal Back Bay into a fashionable residential district, Cambridge sporadically filled small sections of marshland for industry. Concerted efforts to deal with the riverfront did not emerge until the 1880's. Then, the Charles River Embankment Company undertook to fill land and build an embankment between the West Boston (now Longfellow) and Brookline (now Boston University) Bridges; the promoters envisioned a Back Bay-like residential district in the vicinity of a new bridge connecting with Boston's West Chester Park. The bridge (called Harvard Bridge) was completed in 1890, and Massachusetts Avenue was created along its present route east of Lafayette Square, but the fashionable residential district never developed. The Cambridge Park Department took over the work of completing the embankment, followed in 1919 by the Metropolitan District Commission; eventually a parkway was created along the entire Cambridge riverfront. Construction of the Charles River Dam in 1903–1910 stabilized the Basin's water level and ensured the success of the embankment project, which has given Cambridge one of its most important environmental assets.

Although the area around Harvard Bridge did not develop residentially, it became the home early in the 20th century of the Massachusetts Institute of Technology, formerly in Boston. M.I.T. acquired its first Cambridge lands in 1912, began construction of a series of white neoclassic buildings (I13), and moved to Cambridge in 1916. About the same time, Harvard began developing its newly acquired riverfront lands, so that both universities had new facades on the river. Much of the rest of the river (Tour O) developed industrially, generally on an imposing scale. The coming of M.I.T. was important to Cambridge not only in providing the city with another prestigious educational institution but also in attracting—especially since World War II—numerous science- and research-oriented corporations. The presence of M.I.T. has stimulated such developments as Technology Square (H54) and the NASA Electronics Research Center (I1), as well as the apartment complex at 100 Memorial Drive (I8).

By the time of World War I, Cambridge had achieved substantially its present form and land use. Subsequent development has consisted principally of intensification of existing uses, such as the filling in of vacant land in residential districts, the construction of apartment buildings where single-family houses existed, or the substitution of high-rise structures for ones of low density. Housing projects and new industrial buildings have appeared, but university expansion has been more important. Much of the new university construction is noteworthy for its design quality as well as for its size or quantity. Enlightened administrative policy has been responsible, as has the influence of the architectural schools at both institutions. The schools of architecture at Harvard and M.I.T. have brought Cambridge far more than its share of architects living and working in the city, with a resultant influence on institutional and private design. The presence of so many architects' own houses on Tour D (North of Brattle) is one indication of this influence.

Aspects of all phases of Cambridge history are visible on the tours in this guide, from the 17th-century street pattern south of Harvard Square (Tour B) to the space-age developments around M.I.T. (Tour I). The greatest number of buildings included are of the 19th century—appropriately so, because that was the period of the city's most intensive growth. Probably the most important periods architecturally have been the mid-18th century, the later 19th century, and the mid-20th-century—but let the reader judge for himself, using this guide as his aid in assessing the evidence.

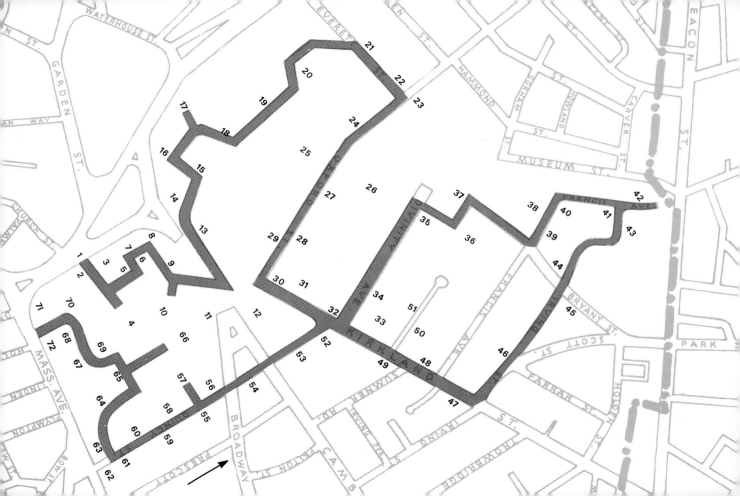

Tour A Harvard Yard and North

The first tour in this guide covers Harvard Yard, the law-science complex to the north, and the Divinity School-Shady Hill district to the east. The oldest and many of the newest Harvard buildings are included, as are the university's principal museums. The tour begins at the Johnston Gate, just north of Harvard Square opposite the Unitarian Church; it ends at Wadsworth House, back in the Square again. Relatively few city streets are traversed in between, because architecturally this is a world unto itself— particularly now that Cambridge Street has been depressed so that the Yard and the law-science buildings to the north form a single continuous area.

Harvard began where the tour begins. Although no 17th-century structures survive, most of Harvard's 18th-century buildings—beginning with Massachusetts Hall of 1718 (A2)— are still very much in use. During the 19th century the college expanded north and east to the present limits of the Yard and a little beyond; the 20th century has brought additional expansion in this direction as well as south (Tour B). Most of the buildings seen on this tour are academic buildings belonging to Harvard; a few 19th-century houses such as Gannett House (A16) have survived in their midst, and one turn-of-the-century residential district, Shady Hill, is visited. Some of Harvard's expansion has been at the expense of good-quality local architecture, but developments such as the moving of the Sparks house (A31) show that enlightened conservation can accompany new construction.

A1

A1 Johnston Gate 1889
McKIM, MEAD & WHITE

This imposing neo-Georgian gateway is the earliest section of McKim, Mead & White's brick-and-iron fencing of Harvard Yard. Donated by various alumni classes and built during the years following 1889, the fencing helped give unity and stature to the Yard's diverse buildings. Harvard's most venerable structures are close by —Massachusetts Hall (A2) on the right, Harvard Hall (A3) on the left, Hollis Hall (A5) and Holden Chapel (A7) out of sight beyond Harvard Hall.

A2 Massachusetts Hall 1718

Gambrel-roofed Massachusetts Hall is the university's oldest existing building. It retains its original exterior form, from brick water table at ground level to dormers and chimneys at the top. The end toward the street is ornamented by a gilded sundial; the opposite end has a door added in the 1930's, when the first story became offices of the university administration. The rest of Massachusetts Hall serves its original function as a dormitory, although it has had several other uses in the course of its long history. During the Revolution the building served as barracks for troops, as did Hollis Hall (A5).

A3 Harvard Hall 1764
GOV. FRANCIS BERNARD, DESIGNER;
THOMAS DAWES, MASTER BUILDER

Built after a fire had destroyed a previous building of the same name on the same site, Harvard Hall originally housed the college library, chapel, dining hall, and classrooms (including a "philosophy chamber" for scientific experiments). The building remains an important example of Georgian architecture, although 19th-century front additions have somewhat obscured its original form. The central three bays, two stories high, were added in 1842; the corner additions, one story high, date from 1870. The rear survives virtually intact. Now serving exclusively for classrooms, Harvard Hall was extensively remodeled in 1968 by Ashley, Myer & Associates.

A4 University Hall 1813

CHARLES BULFINCH

Harvard's first stone building, University Hall is built of Chelmsford granite with wooden Ionic pilasters articulating the entrance bays. A one-story porch that originally extended across the front was removed in 1842 and replaced by two flights of steps; steps were not added on the identical east facade until 1917. Designed to take over some of Harvard Hall's functions of chapel and commons, University Hall now contains administrative offices of the Faculty of Arts and Sciences. The John Harvard statue in front—an ideal portrait, since no likeness of the college's early benefactor is known—is by Daniel Chester French.

A5 Hollis Hall 1762

THOMAS DAWES, MASTER BUILDER

Built as a dormitory and always serving as such, Hollis has been changed (at least on the outside) only in minor ways, such as by having its entrances moved from the Massachusetts Avenue side to the Yard side. 18th-century stylistic characteristics include a brick water table and belt courses between the stories. The interior of Hollis, as of most of the older Yard dormitories, has been remodeled several times, most recently by The Architects Collaborative (1959).

A6 Stoughton Hall 1804

CHARLES BULFINCH, ARCHITECT;
THOMAS DAWES, MASTER BUILDER

Although its massing is copied from Hollis, Stoughton Hall exhibits characteristics of Bulfinch's Federal style— notably the flat wall surfaces. There are no belt courses between stories, and even the granite foundation is virtually flush with the walls. Limestone window lintels replace flat arches of brick; the two entrances are framed in stone instead of wood. Like Hollis, Stoughton Hall is a dormitory.

A7

A7 Holden Chapel 1742
Built as a chapel but used for other purposes since Harvard Hall was opened in 1766, Holden was designed to face the Common rather than the then nonexistent Yard. The elaborate Georgian pediment decoration on the Yard side is 20th-century work, duplicating original work on the opposite gable. In style the building resembles Boston's Faneuil Hall as designed in 1742 (perhaps by John Smibert). Flanking Holden are twin neo-Georgian dormitories, Lionel and Mower Halls (1924, Coolidge, Shepley, Bulfinch & Abbott), built as part of President Lowell's plan to use buildings to wall off the Yard from traffic.

A8 Phillips Brooks House 1898
ALEXANDER WADSWORTH LONGFELLOW, JR.
The design of Phillips Brooks House, built a quarter-century earlier than Lionel and Mower Halls, was inspired by Harvard Hall (A3), the rear of which is visible on the other side of Holden Chapel. The Yard facade of Phillips Brooks House is not the main facade, although it contains the most frequented entrance. The central Palladian window above the entrance lights the landing of a fine oak staircase. The building contains meeting rooms and offices for the university's religious and social-service organizations.

A9 Holworthy Hall 1811
LOAMMI BALDWIN
Following Stoughton's lead stylistically, Holworthy—also a dormitory—goes a step further by eliminating any break in the long facade. Granite is used for sills as well as lintels and for heavy quoined door frames. Engineer-architect Loammi Baldwin had earlier been in charge of construction of the Middlesex Canal (completed 1803), which made Chelmsford granite accessible to Boston builders and architects (such as Bulfinch, who used it in University Hall, A4). Holworthy's roof was raised and the cornice changed later in the 19th century.

A10 Thayer Hall 1869
RYDER & HARRIS

Massive Thayer, another dormitory, joins Holworthy, Hollis, and Stoughton Halls in defining the northern part of the Old Yard. The various sections of the building advance and recede boldly—quite a contrast to the flat, blocklike character of the Yard's early 19th-century structures. Thayer has characteristically heavy Victorian ornament in brown Nova Scotia sandstone.

A11 Hunt Hall 1893
RICHARD MORRIS HUNT

Built as the Fogg Museum of Art, Hunt Hall was renamed for its architect after the present Fogg (A55) opened in 1928. Used since then by the Graduate School of Design, the building fronts on Cambridge Street and has a semicircular rear auditorium that backs up to Memorial Church (A66). North of Hunt Hall and the Yard lies the Cambridge Street Underpass (1967; Charles A. Maguire & Associates, engineers; Sasaki, Dawson, DeMay Associates, landscape architects). To the east, where traffic from the underpass divides, is the Cambridge Fire Department headquarters (1933, Sturgis Associates).

A12 Memorial Hall 1870
WARE & VAN BRUNT

Memorial Hall, which commemorates Harvard men who died during the Civil War, is one of the best examples of Ruskin-influenced architecture in the United States. It holds its own despite loss of the tall, pinnacled roof that originally crowned its central tower. Cathedral-like in shape, the building contains a vast dining hall (no longer used as such) in the "nave," the memorial hall proper (with marble tablets, stained glass, and wooden rib vaulting) in the "transept," and a theater named for Charles Sanders in the "apse." The interiors, still in substantially original condition, are particularly worthy of attention.

A13

A13 Lawrence Hall 1847
RICHARD BOND

This bracketed Italianate structure was built for the Lawrence Scientific School, allied with and later absorbed into Harvard. The wing to the right was originally a residence for the Rumford Professor. In 1870, to enlarge its capacity, Lawrence Hall was gutted inside, and three stories were built where there had been two; at the same time the entrance was moved from the center of the pedimented main block to its present side-porch location. Lawrence's brick is trimmed with brown sandstone above a granite foundation. Corner quoins, round-headed second-story windows, and elaborately projecting stone brackets are noteworthy stylistic features.

A14 Littauer Center 1938
COOLIDGE, SHEPLEY, BULFINCH & ABBOTT

Built of the same Chelmsford granite as Charles Bulfinch's University Hall (A4), neoclassic Littauer (a center for public administration) is copied from another Bulfinch design—the original building of Massachusetts General Hospital (1818). Littauer's six-columned portico terminates an axis from Harvard Square. To the right, backing up to Lawrence Hall, is the Music Building (1913, Howells & Stokes, with a later library addition). Facing Music's pilastered facade across what was once intended to be a tree-lined mall between Massachusetts Avenue and Oxford Street is the Jefferson Physical Laboratory (1884, Shaw & Hunnewell).

A15 Austin Hall 1881
H. H. RICHARDSON

Austin Hall is one of Harvard's—and Richardson's—best buildings. Built for the Law School, Austin has symmetrical one-story classroom wings flanking a main block that originally contained library stacks and offices. A rear wing houses a classroom on the ground floor and a handsome courtroom (originally the library reading room) on the second floor. The building's varied fenestration corresponds to the original function of the rooms inside—high, horizontal banks of windows in the classrooms, vertical strip windows in the book stacks (above the triple-arched portico). Austin's elaborately polychromed masonry is now largely obscured by grime.

A16 Gannett House 1838

This porticoed Greek Revival house, now serving as Law School extra-curricular offices, is the sole survivor of a residential enclave that included the 18th-century Hastings-Holmes house, an important conference center on the eve of the Revolution. Originally facing Harvard Square, Gannett House was turned ninety degrees at the time Littauer was built, forming an axis with the portico of Mallinckrodt Laboratory (A28) at the other end of a now abandoned mall. Hemenway Gymnasium next door (1938) replaces a larger gymnasium of the same name that was demolished for the construction of Littauer.

A17 Walter Hastings Hall 1888
CABOT & CHANDLER

L-shaped Hastings Hall, together with the end of Hemenway Gymnasium, forms a court that opens on the Common. Tawny Roman brick trimmed with brown granite and terra cotta makes this Law School dormitory blend well with its neighbor, Austin Hall. Hastings's steeply pitched slate roof is elaborately trimmed with copper.

A18 Faculty Office Building 1967
BENJAMIN THOMPSON & ASSOCIATES

This new Law School structure, de-signed to accommodate faculty offices, has dark-colored brick to blend with Austin and Hastings Halls and light-colored concrete to blend with Langdell Hall (A19). Another new Law School building by the same firm is going up along Massachusetts Avenue, on the other side of Langdell and the International Legal Studies Center.

A19

A19 Langdell Hall 1906; 1928
SHEPLEY, RUTAN & COOLIDGE; COOLIDGE SHEPLEY, BULFINCH & ABBOTT

Neoclassic Langdell Hall was begun in 1906, several years before M.I.T.'s main complex (I13), its closest stylistic parallel in Cambridge. The southern half was built first; the northern half and an office wing to the west were added two decades later—all in limestone, with a giant order of engaged Ionic columns. The Law School library occupies most of Langdell's second floor; classrooms and administrative offices are on the first floor. A separate structure for the International Legal Studies Center was built in 1957 on the Massachusetts Avenue side (Shepley, Bulfinch, Richardson & Abbott, architects).

A20 Harvard Graduate Center 1949
THE ARCHITECTS COLLABORATIVE (WALTER GROPIUS)

Gropius's Graduate Center was the first appearance at Harvard of forthright modern architecture, in a complex large enough to have considerable impact. Low-slung, clean-lined buildings are grouped around a series of irregular courtyards on various levels and are connected by covered walkways. All the buildings are dormitories except Harkness Commons, which contains dining and meeting rooms. A stainless steel sculpture outside Harkness's curved glass windows is by Richard Lippold; additional works of art (by Arp, Bayer, Miro, and others) are inside the Commons building. Walk through the complex to Everett Street.

A21 27 Everett Street 1890
J. R. & W. P. RICHARDS

The Jarvis is one of Cambridge's earliest apartment houses. Built (as were most local apartment buildings) on a street of single-family houses, it fits in better than most because of its domestic appearance. Its materials are the dark stone and brick of the eighties and nineties (compare Hastings Hall, A17). Although published in *American Architect & Building News* in 1891 The Jarvis generated no local imitators.

A22 White Hall, Lesley College 1957
WILLIAM L. GALVIN

This part of Cambridge is not exclusively a Harvard precinct. Here is a dormitory and dining hall belonging to Lesley College, a women's liberal-arts institution devoted to teacher training. Lesley presently occupies a complex of older frame houses in the vicinity but is about to undertake an ambitious building program oriented around the concept of an "urban academic village." As part of the project, a portion of Mellen Street will be closed off.

A23 Engineering Sciences Laboratory 1962
MINORU YAMASAKI & ASSOCIATES

This pure white cube with shimmering entrance doors belies a utilitarian function as engineering laboratory. The building may seem less anomalous if and when the larger complex of which it is a part is built. For another Yamasaki design, see William James Hall (A33).

A24 Perkins Hall 1893
SHEPLEY, RUTAN & COOLIDGE

Perkins and its companion across Oxford Street (Conant Hall) were Harvard's first Georgian Revival buildings. Designed by the same firm in the same year, Conant is round-bayed, while Perkins is flat-faceded. They are the university's counterpart to the numerous private dormitories that were going up around Harvard Square during the nineties (see Claverly Hall, B39). Beyond Perkins, set back on the right, is Harvard's Computation Center (1946, Coolidge, Shepley, Bulfinch & Abbott; top story, 1964, Shepley, Bulfinch, Richardson & Abbott).

A25

A25 Pierce Hall 1900
SHAW & HUNNEWELL

Science buildings dominate both sides of Oxford Street from here to the intersection of Kirkland Street. Pierce Hall is a laboratory of engineering and applied physics designed by the architects of the Jefferson Physical Laboratory of 1884 (located behind Littauer Center, A14). Built of brick trimmed with limestone (some of it rather elaborately carved), Pierce is sited far enough back from the street so that its mass does not overwhelm the passer-by.

A26 University Museum 1859–1915

Built in several stages by a number of different architects and builders, this massive brick structure comprises the Museum of Comparative Zoology (north wing and northwest corner), the Geological, Mineralogical, and Botanical Museums (center section), and the Peabody Museum of Archaeology and Ethnology (south wing). The wings extend on two sides of a court at the rear of the building (approached from Divinity Avenue); a similar three-sided court is in the process of being created on the front, the Hoffman Laboratory (A27) being one of the wings. Harvard's most frequented tourist attraction, the Ware collection of glass flowers, is housed in the central building of the University Museum.

A27 Hoffman Laboratory 1962
THE ARCHITECTS COLLABORATIVE

Attached to the geological section of the University Museum, this recent structure serves as a laboratory of experimental geology. Built of brick within a concrete structural grid, the building has a solidity and earth-rootedness befitting its function.

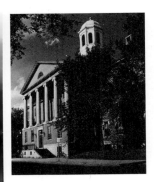

A28 Mallinckrodt Laboratory 1927
COOLIDGE, SHEPLEY, BULFINCH & ABBOTT

Mallinckrodt Laboratory was intended as the terminus of a broad mall leading in from Massachusetts Avenue. Had the mall been completed (it was blocked by construction of Gordon McKay Laboratory, A29), Mallinckrodt's monumental Ionic portico and handsome cupola (copied from the one on Boston's Faneuil Hall) would have had a proper setting. As it is, Mallinckrodt overpowers Oxford Street, and the imposing architectural features seem presumptuous and unnecessary, especially considering the building's utilitarian function as a chemistry laboratory.

A29 Gordon McKay Laboratory 1951
COOLIDGE, SHEPLEY, BULFINCH & ABBOTT

This postwar applied-science laboratory, the top stories of which were added in 1961 by the same firm, carries the glass wall to its Harvard extreme—but compare such contemporary M.I.T. buildings as Dorrance Laboratories (I36). McKay's glass walls are unusual in that they are framed in wood and thus look heavy. At the intersection of Kirkland and Oxford Streets is the site of a forthcoming Science Center by Sert, Jackson and Associates. Ahead is Memorial Hall (A12).

A30 Lowell Lecture Hall 1902
GUY LOWELL

Unlike Hunt Hall (A11), Lowell Lecture Hall (originally known as New Lecture Hall) is named not for its architect but for its long-anonymous donor, Harvard President A. Lawrence Lowell. The building accommodates a large lecture room in its main pilastered mass and a series of tutorial rooms in the basement. Other Harvard buildings by architect Guy Lowell are Emerson Hall (A58) and the President's House (A60).

A31

A31 21 Kirkland Street 1838

WILLIAM SAUNDERS, BUILDER

This conservative, wide-pilastered, Regency/Greek Revival house was built in 1838 at the corner of Quincy and Kirkland Streets for Daniel Treadwell, inventor and Harvard professor. Historian Jared Sparks acquired the house in 1847 and lived there while president of Harvard (1849–1853). Subsequently owned by the New Church Theological School, the property passed in 1966 to Harvard, which moved the house and its stable (now a garage) to this lot. The present siting, with the building's pilastered end facade toward the street and the entrance facade facing the side of the lot, duplicates the original siting.

A32 Busch-Reisinger Museum 1914

GERMAN BESTELMEYER; WARREN & SMITH

Completed in 1917 but not opened until 1921 because World War I was an inauspicious time for a Germanic museum, this stucco-covered, tile-roofed structure by a Munich architect originally contained mainly plaster casts, but its collection has since been expanded to include numerous original works (with emphasis on the 20th century). The next twenty buildings are on a loop that passes through the Shady Hill residential district and returns to this corner. If you wish to follow the Divinity Avenue-Shady Hill loop some other time, skip to A52 (Church of the New Jerusalem) and continue south on Quincy Street.

A33 William James Hall 1963

MINORU YAMASAKI & ASSOCIATES

Fourteen stories of pure white concrete rise up from an open plaza, in aloof disregard of the surroundings. Built of precast piers and wall panels, William James Hall serves as a behavioral sciences center. An off-center utility tower at the rear seems poorly related to the studied symmetrical elegance of the main block.

A34 2 Divinity Avenue 1930
HORACE TRUMBAUER

This late work by Trumbauer has none of the monumentality of his Widener Library (A65). Long and low rather than tall and massive, 2 Divinity has a placid, repetitive facade, adorned by a map of the world above the entrance and by a series of roundels symbolic of the building's original function as the Institute of Geographical Exploration. Attached at the left rear is a handsome and compatible new structure for the Harvard-Yenching Institute (1957, Shepley, Bulfinch, Richardson & Abbott). Beyond is the Semitic Museum (1902, A. W. Longfellow, Jr.).

A35 Divinity Hall 1825

Divinity Hall was the first Harvard building outside the confines of the Yard. Built a decade after University Hall (A4), Divinity is still basically a Federal-style building but has a proto-Greek Revival heaviness of detail . . (especially in the brownstone Doric entrance porches). Originally serving all the functions of the Divinity School (chapel, library, classrooms, and dormitory rooms), the building now serves principally as a dormitory. Across Divinity Avenue is the rear court of the University Museum (A26). The Peabody Museum is on the left, the University Museum proper in the center, and the Museum of Comparative Zoology (begun in 1859) on the right. The new University Herbaria building is a 1953 design by Shepley, Coolidge, Bulfinch & Richardson.

A36 Biological Laboratories 1930
COOLIDGE, SHEPLEY, BULFINCH & ABBOTT

The U-shaped Biological Laboratories echo the three-sided court of the University Museum. Neo-Georgian stylistic features (as on Mallinckrodt Laboratory, A28) have been discarded in favor of a more straightforward, functional approach, although the vertical tiers of metal-framed sash and the basic formality of the design are comparable to other buildings of the early thirties (such as Rindge Technical High School, G8, or the Central Square Post Office, H6). A distinctive feature of the Biological Laboratories is the continuous animal frieze carved in the brick. This frieze and the two rhinoceros statues are by Katherine Ward Lane.

A37

A37 Farlow Herbarium 1886
PEABODY & STEARNS
Now part of the University Herbaria, this building was originally the Divinity Library. From here, the tour route proceeds up and down some stairs between Farlow and the end of the Biological Laboratories, then right toward Francis Avenue. Across a parking lot is visible the grim, bunker-like hulk of the Cambridge Electron Accelerator (1957, Charles T. Main, Inc.). Attached to the rear of Andover Hall (A38) is Shepley, Bulfinch's 1960 Divinity Library addition.

A38 Andover Hall 1910
ALLEN & COLLENS
Built for the Andover Theological Seminary (a separate institution now in Newton) and subsequently acquired by the Harvard Divinity School, this stone Gothic structure, appropriately ecclesiastical in feeling, is the best Cambridge example of Collegiate Gothic—a style ignored at Harvard (unlike Yale and Princeton) in favor of Collegiate Georgian. Allen & Collens were specialists in ecclesiastical work; a more modest Cambridge design of theirs was the 1932 remodeling of St. Peter's Episcopal Church (H4).

A39 Center for the Study of World Religions 1959
SERT, JACKSON & GOURLEY
Like all of José Luis Sert's work, this building is expertly sited. It keeps reappearing from different angles but never dominates the residential neighborhood in which it is located. It serves as a residence and study center associated with the Divinity School.

A40 44 Francis Avenue 1913
DERBY & ROBINSON

This stately brick house is the official residence of the Divinity School dean, although it was privately built for Harvard professor James R. Jewett. Its garage is now a separate dwelling numbered 56 Francis Avenue. Beyond is a grouping of recent houses, including 60 Francis Avenue (1961, Tech-built, Inc.) and 64 Francis Avenue (A41), José Luis Sert's own house. Land in this vicinity was formerly part of an estate called Shady Hill.

A41 64 Francis Avenue 1957
JOSÉ LUIS SERT

No less than three private walled courtyards are part of the plan of this house, which Sert intended to be applicable to row-house situations. Like most inward-turning buildings, the house presents an unassuming exterior (here largely hidden behind a cluster of pines on the Irving Street side) while concentrating on interior spatial and visual effects. Sert was dean of the Harvard Graduate School of Design when he built this house for himself.

A42 67 Francis Avenue 1926
ROBERT P. BELLOWS

The cul-de-sac end of Francis Avenue, beyond the intersection of Irving Street, contains a number of 20th-century houses that revive earlier styles. This one is comparable to Ithiel Town's Federal-style Asa Gray house on Garden Street (E44). Across the street at 68 Francis Avenue is a house more 18th century in inspiration, with center chimney, gable-on-hip roof, and twelve-over-twelve sash in projecting frames.

A43

A43 138 Irving Street 1912
ALLEN W. JACKSON

Next door to this gambrel-roofed, stuccoed, pre-World War I Colonial is vacant land that was the site of Shady Hill, an 1806 Federal-style dwelling demolished by Harvard in 1955. Long owned by Fine Arts professor Charles Eliot Norton, the estate had extensive grounds known as Norton's Woods. Subdivision of the estate began in 1889, following plans by landscape architect Charles Eliot, but this corner (including the site of Andover Hall) was developed only after Norton's death in 1908. 133 Irving Street is a 1963 design by Richard Gallagher. Beyond is another view of Sert's Center for the Study of World Religions (A39).

A44 5 Bryant Street 1916
BIGELOW & WADSWORTH

Now serving as Harvard's Hillel House, this building was originally a private residence. Stylistically similar to 138 Irving (A43), although not so impressively terraced above the street, 5 Bryant belongs to the traditional or Colonial branch of pre-World War I stuccoed houses. Another aspect of the period's Stucco Style is represented by the house diagonally across the intersection of Bryant and Irving (A45).

A45 114 Irving Street 1911
THE CRAFTSMAN

Freer in arrangement and siting than 5 Bryant, this tile-roofed, cement-walled house exemplifies the kind of comfortable, practical, handcrafted house that magazines such as *The Craftsman* promoted in the early years of the 20th century. Often the designs were inspired by medieval or Mediterranean sources, but derivative features are less important than the style's overall character. For a comparable house of the same period by a local architect, see 36 Fresh Pond Parkway (D3). The shingled house next door at 110 Irving Street (1889, William R. Emerson) represents the first period of Shady Hill development; beyond, 104 Irving (1893, Walker & Kimball) was the boyhood home of e.e. cummings.

A46 95 Irving Street 1889
WILLIAM R. EMERSON

William James built this gambrel-roofed shingled house for himself at the outset of Shady Hill's development. Other professors followed, and the character of the district was quickly established. Deed restrictions specified residential use and minimum cost; architects like Emerson established a certain standard of design. The neighborhood has maintained its quality and especially its appeal to Harvard professors down to the present. Next door at 89 Irving Street, facing the side yard, is a three-story white Colonial Revival house designed by J. W. Ames in 1916; other examples of Ames's work may be seen along Brattle Street (114 Brattle, C25; 194 Brattle, D8).

A47 50–60 Kirkland Street 1890
FRANK SHEPARD

This brick block, comparable to some in the further reaches of Boston's Back Bay, is the last gasp of row-house construction in Cambridge. More important for the future were apartment-house designs such as The Jarvis (A21). Although different from its neighbors, the row is set well back from the street, enhancing rather than detracting from its environment. Kirkland Street was one of the earliest traveled routes into Cambridge, part of of the 17th-century "Way from Charlestown to Watertown." In 1830 it was named for Harvard President John T. Kirkland.

A48 1 Francis Avenue 1837

Built for Ebenezer Francis, this early Greek Revival house with 20th-century entrance porch and shingles has a large yard that suggests the spacious feeling of 19th-century Kirkland Street. The original grounds of the house were even larger; Francis Avenue was laid out across them later in the 19th century in a development that coincided with that on the adjoining Norton estate.

A49

A49 38 Kirkland Street 1839
OLIVER HASTINGS AND LUTHER BROOKS, BUILDERS

Comparable to but more elaborate than Gannett House (A16), this temple-fronted Greek Revival dwelling is impressively sited on a terrace above the street. Although the galleried Ionic colonnade is symmetrical, the fenestration behind is not; the front door is slightly off center, allowing wider parlors to the right. Long occupied by Harvard professor Joseph Lovering, then as a nursing home, the house now serves as Harvard offices. The four large outside chimneys are 20th-century additions; the original chimneys were in the same relative positions but were within the walls of the house. Of the three windows in the pediment, only the central one (surmounted by a fan) is original.

A50 4 Kirkland Place 1856
HENRY GREENOUGH

Crowded behind a 1913 apartment building but overlooking its own spacious yard, this brick mansard house originally occupied the entire corner lot extending to Kirkland Street. Although moved and reoriented, it still possesses its original dignity and style. Henry Greenough, who had traveled and studied in Europe with his sculptor brother Horatio, was among the first to introduce the mansard roof to American domestic architecture. Of four known Greenough mansards in Cambridge, this is the only survivor. The house is typically Greenough in being restrained and academically correct, foursquare and symmetrical.

A51 9 Kirkland Place 1855
ISAAC CUTLER, BUILDER

Kirkland Place is a remarkably intact mid-19th-century residential cul-de-sac, many of the houses on which were built by Isaac Cutler. 9 Kirkland Place, the best preserved, is a typical center-gable bracketed house of the fifties.

A52 Church of the New Jerusalem 1903

WARREN, SMITH & BISCOE

This stone Gothic chapel was built for the New Church Theological School (Swedenborgian), which formerly occupied the entire Quincy Street blockfront. After the remainder of the property (including the Jared Sparks house, A31) was sold to Harvard, the church added a wing on Kirkland Street (1966, Arthur H. Brooks, Jr. and Associates).

A53 Gund Hall 1969

JOHN ANDREWS/ANDERSON/BALDWIN

This new building for the Harvard Graduate School of Design is the first Cambridge work by John Andrews, an architect trained at Harvard and practicing from Toronto. Gund Hall will supplant Robinson (A56) and Hunt (A11) in the Yard. The model illustrated above shows the building in a preliminary design stage.

A54 Allston Burr Lecture Hall 1951

COOLIDGE, SHEPLEY, BULFINCH & ABBOTT

Gray glazed brick, smooth curves, and sharp edges characterize this postwar structure built for undergraduate instruction in science under Harvard's General Education program. Inside are two large lecture rooms, their volumes expressed in the raised, curved portions of the exterior massing. Smaller classrooms and offices occupy the rest of the building. An exhibit of historic scientific instruments is displayed in the lobby.

A55

A55 Fogg Art Museum 1925
COOLIDGE, SHEPLEY, BULFINCH & ABBOTT

Harvard neo-Georgian on the outside, the Fogg has a reproduction 16th-century Italian court as its dominant interior feature. Galleries for temporary exhibitions and for portions of the permanent collection surround three sides of the central, top-lighted court; the building also contains lecture rooms, offices, and a library. The original Fogg Museum (A11) was renamed Hunt Hall after this building opened. Across from Fogg's main entrance is a pleasant, tree-shaded quadrangle formed by Robinson, Sever, and Emerson Halls (A56–58).

A56 Robinson Hall 1900
McKIM, MEAD & WHITE

Built for the School of Architecture (about to move to Gund Hall, A53), Robinson Hall is classical in its stylistic references, as befitted the prevailing taste of the architectural profession at the turn of the century. Behind the central part of the facade is a full-height "Great Space," originally a Hall of Casts. Sculptural fragments still adorn the facade, along with plaques inscribed with the names of the architectural gods of the time.

A57 Sever Hall 1878
H. H. RICHARDSON

Built three years before Austin Hall (A15), Sever is another of the university's—and Richardson's—major monuments. Compatible with earlier Yard buildings in being symmetrically planned and built of red brick, Sever departs from precedent in having fenestration keyed to interior function (horizontal banks of windows providing light to classrooms) and in having unique and individualistic brick ornament on all four sides. Other noteworthy features of this classroom building are twin cylindrical towers (corresponding to narrow rooms inside), a high hip roof of orange tile, and a round-arched, deeply recessed entrance on the Yard side.

A58 Emerson Hall 1904
GUY LOWELL

Emerson Hall's greatest virtue is its position on the third side of the Sever Quadrangle. Obviously modeled on McKim, Mead & White's Robinson Hall (A56), Emerson employs similar massing and materials and many of the same architectural devices, such as pilasters and engaged Ionic columns. The interior has been completely redone by The Architects Collaborative, to good advantage.

A59 Carpenter Center for the Visual Arts 1961
LE CORBUSIER; SERT, JACKSON & GOURLEY

Le Corbusier's only building in the United States stands out dramatically from its neighbors, neo-Georgian Fogg (A55) and the Faculty Club (1930, Coolidge, Shepley, Bulfinch & Abbott). It represents a triumph of good design over the limitations of a small, crowded site. Curved sections raised on pilotis project out from the main mass; a stair tower with glass-brick windows provides a vertical accent; brises-soleil or angled sun-baffles modulate the facades; and an open ramp passes through the center of the building. One can walk under, through, and within the Carpenter Center. Accessible from the top of the ramp is an exhibition room; most of the building contains studio space.

A60 President's House 1911
GUY LOWELL

Once Harvard began remaking its image in 20th-century Georgian style, the existing President's House (a cottage-like, mansard-roofed structure built in 1861) was no longer appropriate. In 1911, this three-story brick mansion was constructed next to the 1861 house, which was subsequently demolished. A much earlier President's House survives in Wadsworth House (A72), which accommodated university presidents from 1726 to 1849.

A61

A61 Dana-Palmer House 1822

Recalling the time when Quincy Street was exclusively residential, the Dana-Palmer house today serves as a university guest house. Originally built on the site of Lamont Library (A63), where its columned piazza overlooked Massachusetts Avenue, the house was moved to its present location in 1946. Basically a hip-roofed Federal-style house, the building has undergone a number of changes, including a period when it served as the Harvard Observatory and had a telescope dome on its roof. Toward Prescott Street stands another survival from the past, Warren House (1833), which was moved back to make room for the Harvard Union (A62) and now serves as English Department offices.

A62 Harvard Union 1900
McKIM, MEAD & WHITE

McKim, Mead & White's Union, predictably Georgian Revival in style, has a monumental paneled dining room inside. The building was completely symmetrical until the present Varsity Club wing was built in 1911 (Thomas Mott Shaw, architect). The Union serves as a freshman dining hall and social center.

A63 Lamont Library 1947
COOLIDGE, SHEPLEY, BULFINCH & ABBOTT

This undergraduate library was Harvard's first major postwar building, preceding the Graduate Center (A20). More important for its open-stack planning than for its stylistic character, Lamont is a kind of compromise between "traditional" and "modern." The Woodberry Poetry Room inside was designed by Alvar Aalto. Between Lamont and the President's House, a mammoth underground library is being built to supplement the facilities of Lamont, Houghton (A64), and Widener (A65) Libraries.

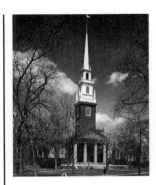

A64 Houghton Library 1941
PERRY, SHAW & HEPBURN

Houghton Library makes no attempt to look modern, although it was given the most advanced humidity and temperature control system available, befitting its function as a rare book library. The building's carefully proportioned bow-fronted facade faces Quincy Street; its more utilitarian rear is attached by a bridge to the side of Widener Library (A65). The interiors are sumptuously finished.

A65 Widener Library 1913
HORACE TRUMBAUER

Massive Widener, the main university library, appropriately dominates the Yard. It replaces an earlier, smaller library—Gore Hall, a turreted Gothic Revival structure built in 1838. The open space between Widener and Memorial Church (A66) is the Yard's largest; known as the Tercentenary Theatre, it is the setting for Harvard Commencements. Inside Widener, dioramas depict Harvard Square at three points in time—1667, 1775, and 1936. A Widener memorial room contains the book collection of Harry Elkins Widener, in whose memory the building was donated. In the main stair hall are murals by John Singer Sargent.

A66 Memorial Church 1931
COOLIDGE, SHEPLEY, BULFINCH & ABBOTT

Memorial Church occupies the site of Appleton Chapel, an 1856 Roman-esque structure. The building has two substantial Doric porticoes intended to balance the mass of Widener. One portico faces the rear of Thayer Hall (A10) and serves as the main entrance; the other faces Widener and leads to a memorial to Harvard men who died in World War I. From a tower above the memorial room soars a steeple modeled on Boston's Christ Church (Old North Church). The chancel of Memorial Church, to the right, is named Appleton Chapel after the earlier building.

A67

A67 Boylston Hall 1857
SCHULTZE & SCHOEN

Boylston Hall has had three important building periods—1857, when the initial structure was built; 1871, when the mansard roof was added; and 1959, when (after complete gutting) the present interior was designed by The Architects Collaborative. Massive granite ashlar masonry and large round-arched openings (enhanced by unobstructed plate glass) set Boylston apart from the surrounding red-brick Yard buildings. Long used as a science laboratory, Boylston is now a Modern Languages Center. In front, toward Widener Library, a Chinese Ch'ing Dynasty sculpture recalls that Boylston Hall once housed the Harvard-Yenching Institute, now at 2 Divinity Avenue (A34).

A68 Grays Hall 1862
N. J. BRADLEE

Three Victorian dormitories define the southern half of the Old Yard. Grays Hall, the central building of the three, opposes distant Holworthy Hall (A9). Built a decade earlier than its neighbors Weld Hall (A69) and Matthews Hall (A70), Grays is trimmed with granite and has a projecting center pavilion and a simple mansard roof. Behind Grays and Boylston Halls and Widener Library is Wigglesworth Hall (1930, Coolidge, Shepley, Bulfinch & Abbott) —three sections of neo-Georgian dormitory interspersed by gates and passageways leading to Massachusetts Avenue.

A69 Weld Hall 1870
WARE & VAN BRUNT

Built of brick trimmed with Nova Scotia sandstone, Weld shares a number of characteristics with its contemporary, Matthews Hall (A70)— materials, massing, steeply pitched roof, variety in bays and projections. Distinctive to Weld Hall, which was designed by the architects of Memorial Hall (A12), are its robust Jacobean gables and its two high glazed towers intended to provide light to interior stairwells. Although Grays, Weld, and Matthews Halls are different in style from the buildings at the north end of the Yard, their basic similarity in scale, material, and placement maintains a harmonious relationship, helping to make the Old Yard one of the most successful open spaces of its size in the country.

A70 Matthews Hall 1871

PEABODY & STEARNS

Matthews is even more exuberant than Weld Hall, with precipitously steep gables and elaborately ornamented projecting entrance porches. Behind Matthews lies a pleasant courtyard bounded by the rear of Massachusetts Hall (A2) and by Straus Hall (1925, Coolidge, Shepley, Bulfinch & Abbott).

A71 Lehman Hall 1924

COOLIDGE, SHEPLEY, BULFINCH & ABBOTT

Built at the same time as Straus, Lionel, Mower, and Wigglesworth Halls under President Lowell's plan to wall off the Yard with buildings, Lehman Hall turns its back on Massachusetts Avenue and opens inward. Although it plays an important role in defining the space of Harvard Square, its only entrances are on the Yard side. Formerly the university comptroller's office, the building now serves as Dudley House, a center for commuting students. A Henry Moore sculpture on loan from the Fogg Museum adorns the brick-paved, beech-shaded courtyard in front.

A72 Wadsworth House 1726

Built as an official residence for Harvard presidents, this 18th-century house was first occupied by President Benjamin Wadsworth, after whom it is named. While other landmarks of pre-Revolutionary Harvard Square have disappeared (such as the meeting house that stood near where Lehman Hall is), Wadsworth House survives— its domestic character incongruous but welcome, its authentically Georgian features a good point of comparison with all its neo-Georgian neighbors. Not used as a President's House since 1849, Wadsworth now contains alumni offices. Tour A ends here in Harvard Square, within sight of the subway kiosk where Tour B begins.

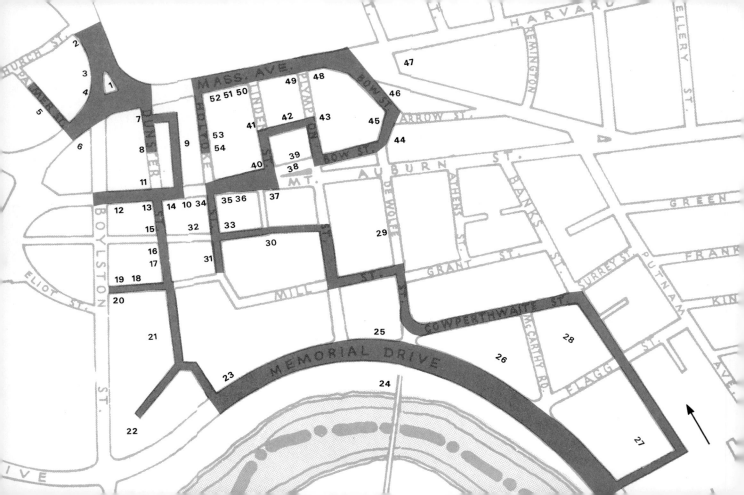

Tour B Harvard Square and South

Tour B begins in Harvard Square and follows a meandering route southeast as far as Peabody Terrace (B27). Included on the tour are commercial buildings, surviving private houses, private dormitories, Harvard Houses, and clubhouses—in approximately equal quantity. The part of the tour route closest to Harvard Square was the first settled part of Cambridge, but nothing remains from that earliest period except a portion of the street pattern and a small park (Winthrop Square) that originally served as a market place. Two 18th-century houses survive—the John Hicks house (B20) and Apthorp House (B42)—but one has been moved and the other surrounded by later buildings. Some 19th-century architecture remains, but the most significant build-ings are those of the 20th century, when Harvard remade the riverfront with a series of imposing neo-Georgian dormitories, followed in more recent years by high-rise structures both along the river (Peabody Terrace, B27) and close to the Square (Holyoke Center, B9). The tour therefore offers considerable variety, both architectural and environmental—an interesting mix of old, fairly recent, and new, in an area where development has by no means ceased.

B1

B1 Subway Kiosk 1928
The focus of Harvard Square is this unassuming subway kiosk, the second one on this spot since the subway was opened in 1912. The first head house was larger—a columned brick structure, oval in plan. It was taken down because it was thought to impair visibility from passing automobiles (already a Harvard Square problem in 1928). This objection seems not to have held when the present prefabricated Out-of-Town Newsstand (built 1966) was approved. In connection with MBTA expansion, the subway entrance will be moved elsewhere; perhaps then the center of Harvard Square can be made less chaotic.

B2 College House 1845–1859
Originally a Harvard dormitory with stores on the ground floor, College House has undergone additions, alterations, and reductions in length. The first section (now demolished) was built in 1832 where Harvard Trust stands; the next section (up to where the facade changes direction) was added in 1845; and the final section (extending to Church Street) was built in 1859. The building originally had a simple pitched roof without dormers: in 1870 a central fourth story and a mansard roof were added. College House was converted to offices in the 1920's, when the University (now Harvard Square) Theatre was built behind.

B3 Harvard Trust Company 1956
PERRY, SHAW, HEPBURN & DEAN
Incorporating an older building behind the left portion of its facade, and providing retail space for the Harvard Coop as well as facilities for the bank, this building solves a complex architectural problem in an orderly if unexciting way. Adjustable vertical aluminum blinds provide a measure of flexibility within the rigid facade grid.

B4 Harvard Cooperative Society 1924

PERRY, SHAW & HEPBURN

Three decades before Harvard Trust's new facade was commissioned, the same architectural firm designed this building for the Coop. At the time, neo-Georgian was the only acceptable style for a Harvard-connected organization. A new marquee shared with the bank is an environmental asset, although the letters carrying across from one building to the next detract from the symmetry of the facade.

B5 Palmer Street

Through paving and planting designed by landscape architects Moriece & Gary, an unsightly alley has been transformed into an inviting pedestrian way —unfortunately but necessarily also serving as a loading zone for the Coop. A two-story glass-enclosed bridge connects the back of the old Coop building with a new bookstore annex (1964, Samuel Glaser Associates). Terminating the view at Church Street is a gabled brick structure built in 1864 as a city police station.

B6 Abbot Building 1909

NEWHALL & BLEVINS

Built for the late Edwin Abbot, whose house is now the Longy School of Music (E25), this commercial block stands on a triangular lot that survives from Cambridge's 17th-century street pattern. To the left, Boylston Street leads toward the river, where the Larz Anderson Bridge occupies the site of Cambridge's "Great Bridge" of 1660. To the right, Brattle Street angles into Brattle Square; just beyond, at the Cambridge Center for Adult Education, is the starting point of Tour C.

B7

B7 Cambridge Savings Bank 1923
NEWHALL & BLEVINS

Most of Harvard Square was rebuilt in a Georgian vein in the twenties. The university built Straus Hall and Lehman Hall (A71); the Coop built its building (B4); and the Cambridge Savings Bank built this structure to replace its prior home around the corner (B8). Newhall & Blevins designed much of the city's speculative, commercial, and civic architecture during the first quarter of the century. To the right, rounding the corner of Boylston Street, a gray-painted wooden facade (1896, J. R. & W. P. Richards) unifies several earlier buildings.

B8 Reliance Cooperative Bank 1897
C. H. BLACKALL

The upper floors of this elaborately ornamented limestone-and-white-brick building originally served as a private dormitory called Dana Chambers. The ground story has always housed shops and a bank. Reliance Cooperative carries on the banking function from the Cambridge Savings Bank, which built the building.

B9 Holyoke Center 1961–1965
SERT, JACKSON & GOURLEY

One of the most ambitious and successful of Harvard's recent building projects, Holyoke Center integrates a variety of functions (shops, offices, medical center, garage) into a single coherent structure covering an entire city block. The H-shaped main mass is ten stories high, but because of its setback it does not overwhelm the surrounding streets. Forbes Plaza expands the space of Harvard Square; a pedestrian arcade through the center of the block leads south toward the river. Follow the central walkway through to Mt. Auburn Street.

B10 78 Mt. Auburn Street 1839

This modest Greek Revival house recalls the residential character of the Mt. Auburn Street district before Harvard's expansion to the south. Like many other houses in the vicinity, it is now owned by Harvard and used for offices.

B11 79 Mt. Auburn Street 1860

Now a story higher and with its arched openings bricked up, this building originally served as a stable and car barn for the Union Railway Company, predecessor of the MBTA in the days of horse-drawn streetcars. Converted to an automobile garage in 1917, the building now connects with the Harvard Square Garage, entered from Boylston Street. The goldsmith's shop at the corner suggests a possible conversion of the Dunster Street arcade to a series of shops, complementing those across the street in Holyoke Center.

B12 44 Boylston Street 1906
GUY LOWELL

This 20th-century clubhouse faces Winthrop Square, a small park that was the town market place during the 17th and 18th centuries. Domestic in appearance like most Harvard clubhouses, the Fox Club is unusual in being built of frame construction. It is now covered with aluminum clapboards—a successful application of modern siding because the building's original trim (pilasters, cornice, window and door frames) was all retained. Diagonally across Winthrop Square is the Pi Eta Club (1908, Putnam & Cox).

B13

B13 45 Dunster Street 1930
PERRY, SHAW & HEPBURN

This district was the heart of 17th-century Cambridge, built up with steep-roofed, clapboarded houses in modest gardens. The first Cambridge meeting house (1632) stood here, as noted by a plaque on the corner. Successive waves of rebuilding have occurred throughout the district, so that now the earliest buildings are the few that survive from the 19th century. This neo-Georgian structure, built in 1930, has a retail store on the ground floor but serves principally as the D.U. clubhouse.

B14 46 Dunster Street 1820
DANIEL DASCOMB, HOUSEWRIGHT

This modest Federal house has undergone several additions and alterations, including Georgian Revival facade ornament added by Bertram Goodhue and Pierre LaRose in 1902, when the building was converted for use by the Signet Society (a Harvard literary association). Next door at 54 Dunster Street, a former Harvard clubhouse (1900, A. J. Russell) now houses university offices.

B15 53 Dunster Street 1841
WILLIAM SAUNDERS & STEPHEN S. BUNKER, HOUSEWRIGHTS

Although built on the standard side-hall plan, this Greek Revival house with south-facing piazza is unusual in being a full three stories in height. A building contract for the house survives, giving insight into mid-19th-century construction methods. In commendably original condition, the house now serves as the Master's Residence for Harvard's Dudley House.

B16 University Lutheran Church 1950

ARLAND DIRLAM

Cambridge's first postwar church is the only recent non-Harvard structure in the vicinity. Although the detail is simple and nonarchaeological, the massing is Romanesque in feeling (compare St. Paul's Church, B44). Across Dunster Street is Harvard's Indoor Athletic Building, seen again later on the tour (B31).

B17 69 Dunster Street 1829

OLIVER HASTINGS, BUILDER

A holdover from an earlier era, when the district was filled with single-family houses. The late 19th-century frame building next door at 77 Dunster (now Harvard offices) represents a subsequent era of multifamily dwellings; college buildings represent the present era. A granite tablet marks the corner of Dunster and South Streets as the site of Harvard President Henry Dunster's house in the 17th century.

B18 17 South Street 1826

Another survival from earlier times, this cottage preserves the scale and setting if not the form and style of Cambridge's first period. The wood shingles and two-over-two windows are replacements for clapboards and six-over-six sash. Next door at 21 South Street is the *Harvard Advocate* building (Eric Kabbon, 1956).

B19

B19 60 Boylston Street 1929
SMITH & WALKER

This neo-Georgian gambrel-roofed structure, built as a fraternity house, now serves as headquarters for the Harvard Department of Athletics. It makes a pleasant contrast with its modest but authentic neighbor across South Street (B20).

B20 64 Boylston Street 1762

The John Hicks house is the only 18th-century building south of Mt. Auburn Street. Moved from the corner of Dunster and Winthrop Streets when the Indoor Athletic Building (B31) was built, it now serves as the library of Kirkland House, from which it is entered. Across Boylston Street toward the river are the MBTA car yards, future site of I. M. Pei's Kennedy Library. The tour now proceeds back along South Street and right on Dunster, past the Kirkland House Master's Residence.

B21 Kirkland House 1913
SHEPLEY, RUTAN & COOLIDGE

Smith Halls, which surround Kirkland's main quadrangle, were among the first units constructed under Harvard's program for building on land near the river. Built as freshman dormitories, they have housed upperclassmen since the establishment of the House system in 1930, when Bryan Hall and the Master's Residence were added by Coolidge, Shepley, Bulfinch, & Abbott, and the John Hicks house (B20) became Kirkland's library. Each Harvard House contains residential quarters, dining room, library, and common rooms for several hundred upperclass students and tutors. The same architectural firm (its name changing slightly over the years) has designed or adapted all the Houses.

B22 Eliot House 1930
COOLIDGE. SHEPLEY. BULFINCH & ABBOTT

Three of the original seven Harvard Houses, including Eliot, were built from scratch, not incorporating preexisting structures. Eliot House is built around a polygonal central courtyard that opens to the river through a handsome iron gate. Over the portion of the building containing the dining hall rises a tower with cupola derived from the one on New York's City Hall (1802). All the Houses were named for Harvard presidents—Eliot for Charles W. Eliot, president from 1869 to 1909. Since the Eliot gate is usually locked, the tour approaches the river between the two buildings of Winthrop House (B23).

B23 Winthrop House 1913
SHEPLEY, RUTAN & COOLIDGE

The two units of Winthrop House, Standish Hall (the one nearer Eliot House) and Gore Hall, were built as freshman dormitories, later were converted to House use. They were the first Harvard buildings to open up to the river. The courtyard facade of Gore Hall (illustrated here) was inspired by Hampton Court Palace as rebuilt by Sir Christopher Wren in the late 17th century.

B24 Weeks Bridge 1926
McKIM, MEAD & WHITE

Harvard Georgian extends across the river in this graceful footbridge that links the Cambridge side of the Charles with the Business School (O19). Besides carrying pedestrians, the Weeks Bridge carries steam pipes to the Business School. The bridge was originally embellished with ornamental bronze light standards, unfortunately destroyed by vandals.

B25

B25 Leverett House Library and Towers 1959

SHEPLEY, BULFINCH, RICHARDSON & ABBOTT

Leverett Towers were Harvard's first high-rise buildings. Grouped with them is the Leverett library, a separate pavilion with a parasol roof. Across DeWolfe Street is the older part of Leverett House—McKinlock Hall, built in 1925 as a freshman dormitory and enlarged in 1930 when the House system came into operation.

B26 Dunster House 1929

COOLIDGE, SHEPLEY, BULFINCH & ABBOTT

Dunster is another of the three original Houses built all of a piece. The site is a triangle, to which the building responds by sending out a myriad of little wings from the main tower-capped block. The wing farthest to the right is the Master's Residence, numbered 935 Memorial Drive.

B27 Peabody Terrace 1963

SERT, JACKSON & GOURLEY

Peabody Terrace is a residential complex for married Harvard students. Strikingly sited along the river, it consists of three twenty-two-story towers, various connecting lower buildings, a garage, and several courtyards. A broad brick-paved walkway through the center of the complex connects the King School neighborhood with the river. Skip-stop elevator design and balconies with sun-baffles are among the features of the towers, which contain apartments of one to five rooms. A walk through Peabody Terrace is rewarded by a variety of vistas, from intimate to open and exhilarating. Follow Banks Street back toward the Harvard Houses.

B28 Mather House 1967
SHEPLEY, BULFINCH, RICHARDSON & ABBOTT

Harvard's newest House, like adjacent Dunster, occupies a triangular site, but it takes its cue more from Peabody Terrace in combining a high-rise tower with lower surrounding buildings.

B29 Quincy House 1958
SHEPLEY, BULFINCH, RICHARDSON & ABBOTT

Quincy initiated a new wave of Harvard House construction, the first since the thirties. The building breaks with the Georgian tradition but uses red brick as its principal material. A library pavilion and dining room wing are attached on the Plympton Street side. In the same block is Mather Hall (1930, Coolidge, Shepley, Bulfinch & Abbott), originally part of Leverett House but annexed to Quincy when Leverett Towers (B25) were opened.

B30 Lowell House 1929
COOLIDGE, SHEPLEY, BULFINCH & ABBOTT

Lowell is the third of the three original Houses built all at once. The site is more regular than those of Eliot House (B22) or Dunster House (B26), but the neo-Georgian style is the same. Two rectangular courtyards—the main one terraced—and a tower inspired by Independence Hall are noteworthy features of Lowell. The interior of the dining hall, which forms the lower side of the main court, is a particularly fine example of Harvard's neo-Georgian opulence.

B31

B31 Indoor Athletic Building 1929
COOLIDGE, SHEPLEY, BULFINCH & ABBOTT
Similar in style to the Harvard Houses,
which were created at the same time,
the Indoor Athletic Building dominates
its residential neighbors. The building
contains gymnasia, a swimming pool,
and related facilities. As a plaque on
the corner indicates, Theodore
Roosevelt lived on this site as a student;
the house he occupied was in scale
with the one that survives across
Winthrop Street (B32).

B32 41 Winthrop Street 1845
An anachronism that benefits from an
open grass plot at the corner, formerly
occupied by other houses. Greek
Revival pilasters and entablature mark
this simple house as a product of the
1840's.

B33 30 Holyoke Street 1905
JAMES PURDON
The Owl Club is a brick neo-Georgian
structure that predates its neighbor,
Lowell House, by a quarter-century.
Harvard clubs (a number of which
originated as fraternities) infiltrated the
district south of Mt. Auburn Street
before the university proper did.
Initially the clubs took over existing
dwellings; when they became prosperous enough, they built new clubhouses, often on the same sites.

B34 76 Mt. Auburn Street 1931
WILLIAM T. ALDRICH

The Spee Club occupies the newest of Harvard clubhouses; it and the D.U. Clubhouse (B13) are the only ones built since World War I. Mt. Auburn Street is the center of club life; all the clubs have their buildings on the street or within a block of it. The location is a holdover from the "Gold Coast" days of the late 19th and early 20th centuries, when luxurious private dormitories such as Claverly and Randolph Halls (B39–40) housed the wealthy students who were also club members.

B35 74 Mt. Auburn Street 1916
WARREN & WETMORE

The Iroquois clubhouse was inspired by Boodles Club in London. Warren & Wetmore, a New York firm, had previously designed the New York Yacht Club, Grand Central Terminal, and other notable structures, plus a private dormitory in Cambridge (Westmorly Court, B45). Clubs are not as important a part of Harvard undergraduate life as fraternities are at many colleges, since only about ten percent of Harvard students are members, but they are important to those who belong to them, and their substantial buildings give evidence of the loyalty of their graduates.

B36 72 Mt. Auburn Street 1915
COOLIDGE & SHATTUCK

The Phoenix-S.K. Club is neo-Georgian rather than Adamesque like its neighbor, Iroquois. The two attached structures offer little in the way of architectural congruity; each makes its own independent statement.

B37

B37 2 Holyoke Place 1899–1902
H. D. HALE

The Fly Club is oriented with its step-gabled end toward Mt. Auburn Street. The curious blocky capitals on the portico columns are substitutes for decayed Corinthian capitals. A large yard behind the Fly Club provides welcome breathing space in this built-up district.

B38 *Lampoon* Building 1909
WHEELWRIGHT & HAVEN

The *Lampoon* "castle" is one of the city's landmark buildings. Taking perfect advantage of its triangular site, it is a whimsical building appropriate to the conduct of a humor magazine's affairs. Architecturally, it puts the *Harvard Crimson* building (B43) to shame—perhaps one reason why *Crimson* staffers repeatedly abscond with the *Lampoon's* mascot, the ibis statue atop the corner tower.

B39 Claverly Hall 1892
GEORGE FOGERTY

Now owned by Harvard, Claverly Hall was originally a private dormitory—part of the "Gold Coast" where wealthy students lived. The building is monumental in scale, with rounded corner bays, a two-story arched entrance, and a heavy classical cornice. Next door at 65 Mt. Auburn Street, another private dormitory (Ridgely Hall, 1904, George S. R. McLean) is now a nonuniversity apartment building. Beyond, Manter Hall School dates from 1927 (Charles Way, architect).

B40 Randolph Hall 1897
COOLIDGE & WRIGHT

Also built as a private dormitory, Jacobean-gabled Randolph is now part of Harvard's Adams House. U-shaped in plan, the building occupies the front yard of historic Apthorp House (B42).

B41 9 Linden Street 1902
JAMES PURDON

The Delphic Club is similar in style to the same architect's Owl Club (B33), built three years later. Across Linden Street is an entrance to the courtyard of Randolph Hall, where Apthorp House is hidden.

B42 Apthorp House 1760

Comparable in size, style, and social origins to the Tory mansions of Brattle Street, Apthorp House was built by East Apthorp, first minister of Christ Church (E3). Without its later third story, it is nearly identical to the Vassall house (C19); possibly the design was provided by Christ Church's architect, Peter Harrison. Dubbed the "Bishop's Palace," Apthorp House was suspect in predominantly Congregational pre-Revolutionary Cambridge; in less than four years, Apthorp left for England. Originally sited on spacious terraced grounds overlooking the river, the house is now encircled by later buildings. It serves as the Adams House Master's Residence.

B43

B43 14 Plympton Street 1915
JARDINE, HILL & MURDOCK

Although not up to the standard of the college's neo-Georgian architecture, the *Crimson* building has the same stylistic roots. To the right is a part of Adams House built in 1931, when several private dormitories were consolidated into Adams. On the corner, cupola-crowned Russell Hall (Adams C-entry) replaces a Gold Coast dormitory of the same name. The tour proceeds to the left up Bow Street toward the side of St. Paul's Church (B44).

B44 St. Paul's Church 1915
EDWARD T. P. GRAHAM

A tall campanile is the dominant feature of this Catholic church modeled on the Italian Romanesque. The source for the campanile was the Torre del Commune in Verona; for the church proper, S. Zeno Maggiore. Extensive cast-stone ornament enriches the facade, which faces a small, irregularly shaped square (rather Italian in feeling itself) at the intersection of Bow and Arrow Streets. St. Paul's School next door occupies an 1889 building by Patrick Ford. Behind, St. Paul's Rectory at 32–36 Mt. Auburn Street is, like the church, by Edward T. P. Graham.

B45 Westmorly Court 1898–1902
WARREN & WETMORE

Now part of Adams House, this luxurious private dormitory was built in two stages—Westmorly Court South (Adams B-entry) in 1898, Westmorly Court North (A-entry) in 1902. Among the building's amenities is a swimming pool.

B46 1218 Massachusetts Avenue 1891

GEORGE FOGERTY

This "flatiron" building, Quincy Hall, was the first private dormitory by George Fogerty, soon to design Claverly (B39). and Ware (G5). Unlike those later, more symmetrical structures, Quincy Hall still has irregular features of the Queen Anne style, including a cylindrical, copper-clad corner bay and a mildly Richardsonian entrance arch. No longer a dormitory, 1218 is now an apartment building.

B47 Quincy Square Gulf Station 1940

GULF OIL CORPORATION

Choosing a "Colonial" theme, Gulf's architects did their best to make this cupola-crowned gas station a dignified part of the Harvard scene. Gas stations are normally short-lived; this one may soon be replaced by a parking garage. A previous building—much more massive—on this trapezoidal site was Beck Hall (1876, N. J. Bradlee), one of the first of the luxurious private dormitories that gave rise to the "Gold Coast" appellation. Tour G (Dana Hill) begins beyond, at the Old Cambridge Baptist Church.

B48 1246–1260 Massachusetts Avenue 1902

COOLIDGE & CARLSON

Beaux Arts in its eclecticism, this elaborately ornamented granite-and-brick structure has stores on the ground floor and apartments (entered from Plympton Street) on the five upper floors. Like so many other Harvard Square buildings of the period, it was designed as a private dormitory.

B49

B49 1268–1270 Massachusetts Avenue 1899

CUMMINGS & PARKER

The A.D. Club occupies the upper floors of this handsomely detailed limestone-and-brick structure, which has commercial space on the ground story. Pilastered like its neighbor across Plympton Street (B48), the building is more restrained and unified in design, besides being less overpowering in height.

B50 1300–1316 Massachusetts Avenue 1869–1885

Three buildings of varying dates are united by a broad copper cornice and share a common entrance to the upper floors, which are apartments. The corner building, dating from 1869, was originally mansard-roofed; pedimented window lintels of Nova Scotia sandstone survive to suggest the structure's former French Second Empire glory. The adjoining building, six windows wide, was built (as a plaque above the fourth story indicates) in 1883; the right-hand building, four windows wide and also dated on the facade, was added in 1885. The block preserves two fine store fronts—1304 (B51) and 1316 Massachusetts Avenue.

B51 1304 Massachusetts Avenue 1907

COOLIDGE & CARLSON

Still intact down to the hardware on the door, the curvaceous facade of Felix's newsstand is Cambridge's only example of Art Nouveau and one of the surprise delights of Harvard Square. It is illustrated here in an old photograph, taken when the shop was a shoe store. A few doors down, Leavitt & Peirce's store front at 1316 Massachusetts Avenue is older (dating from the time the building was put up in 1885) and just as intact. Run-of-the-mill when built, it has survived several waves of change to become a valuable period piece.

B52 1320–1324 Massachusetts Avenue 1890

W. Y. PETERS

Brown Roman brick was used for the austere facade of the Porcellian Club, which is original (except for J. August's sign) down to the ground-story store. The shop front, the entrance door to the clubrooms, and the window above are detailed in a delicate, Federal-style manner—a foretaste of the emerging Federal Revival.

B53 12 Holyoke Street 1887

PEABODY & STEARNS

Although less distinguished architecturally than the Porcellian building, the Hasty Pudding clubhouse is worthy of note for its round-arched ground-story windows and its diamond-ornamented bracketed eaves. The oldest collegiate society in the country (by virtue of its association with the Institute of 1770), the Hasty Pudding Club is best known for its annual theatricals (a Harvard institution since 1844), held in a hall at the rear of the building.

B54 Apley Court 1897

JOHN E. HOWE

Now part of Dudley House, Apley Court is a final private dormitory on this tour that has included so many. Solidly neo-Georgian in brick and limestone, the building is ornamented by window and door grilles that are almost rococo in feeling. Across the street, embedded in the sidewalk, a granite plaque marks the site of the first Cambridge school house. A walk past some of Holyoke Center's shops leads one back to Harvard Square, where the tour began.

Tour C Brattle Street

Brattle is Cambridge's most famous street, notable for both its history and its architecture. It begins amid the commercial bustle of Harvard Square, then winds its way past educational and religious buildings before becoming purely residential, a character it maintains for the remainder of its length. Tour C traverses Brattle Street from the house of William Brattle (now the Cambridge Center for Adult Education) to the intersection of Elmwood Avenue, then turns on Elmwood to follow the route of the old highway to Watertown. (The section of Brattle Street beyond Elmwood Avenue was not opened until the 19th century.) Most of the city's notable pre-Revolutionary houses are included on the tour; the fact that the majority of them were owned by Loyalists gave Brattle Street its nickname, Tory Row. The street's present character results from 19th-century subdivision of the pre-Revolutionary estates. Occasional new houses were built in the first three-quarters of the 19th century, but the most intensive development occurred in the 1880's. 20th-century construction has been on the sites of earlier buildings—usually two or three new houses where formerly there was one Tour C ends at Elmwood Avenue and Mt. Auburn Street, where busses are available to Harvard Square. The beginning of Tour D (a walking route back to the Square) is only a few blocks away.

C1

C1 42 Brattle Street 1727
Brattle Street takes its name from the family that lived in this gambrel-roofed house during the 18th century. Built for Loyalist William Brattle, the house is the first in a series of Tory Row mansions extending to Elmwood (C54). Except for the projecting entrance porch (added around 1890), the front part of the house is largely authentic. Inside, original woodwork survives only on the staircase and in the right downstairs room. The Cambridge Social Union (parent organization of the Cambridge Center for Adult Education) acquired the property in 1889 and built Brattle Hall (now the Brattle Theatre) next door.

C2 46 Brattle Street 1966
THE ARCHITECTS COLLABORATIVE
The Architects Collaborative has its offices in this building, which is set back from Brattle Street and entered from a sunken brick plaza. Another entrance is on Story Street. The quality of the TAC building is a welcome relief from the banality of most of the commercial architecture on this part of Brattle Street. The corner of Brattle and Story Streets is the site of a new Design Research building by Benjamin Thompson & Associates.

C3 54 Brattle Street 1808
Now sandwiched between an office building and an apartment house, the Window Shop was once the home of Dexter Pratt, Longfellow's village blacksmith. Pratt's shop stood next door, toward Story Street, with the legendary spreading chestnut tree at the curb. The restaurant building is a simple, two-story, hip-roofed Federal house; the glass-walled shop at the rear was added in 1946 by architects Kennedy & Johnson. A canopy in front provides shelter for outside dining. Most of the interior of the house has been changed, but the original three-run staircase still exists.

C4 Read House ca. 1772

James Read, who built this house just prior to the Revolution, was a patriot rather than a Loyalist. Simpler in style than Cambridge's Tory mansions (compare its almost crude staircase with the elegant one at the Brattle house, C1), the Read house nonetheless possesses an elaborate classical door frame, copied from an English 18th-century pattern book (Batty Langley, *City and Country Builder,* 1740). Harvard University is preserving the house by moving it to a nearby corner of the School of Education Library site; look for it off Farwell Place if it is not at its original location, 55 Brattle.

C5 Nichols House 1827

OLIVER HASTINGS, BUILDER

This early 19-century dwelling is distinguished by its two bow-fronted bays that project under a Tuscan-columned front porch. Inside, a graceful curving staircase rises to the second floor. Harvard is moving the Nichols house from 63 Brattle Street to a corner of the Education Library site adjacent to the Read house. Benjamin Thompson & Associates are the architects of the new library and research center.

C6 Loeb Drama Center 1959

HUGH STUBBINS & ASSOCIATES

Harvard's undergraduate theatre was located here so that it would be equally convenient to Harvard students, Radcliffe students, and the general public. Suspended metal grilles adorn the facades of the building, which has a serpentine-walled garden overlooking the lawn of 76 Brattle (C7). Across the street, two early houses survive in what is now the Radcliffe Yard. 69 and 77 Brattle Street date respectively from 1838 and 1821. Buildings in the Radcliffe Yard are seen on the Garden Street tour (E6—11).

C7

C7 76 Brattle Street 1859

A commodious mansard-roofed mansion set in spacious grounds, Greenleaf House has served since 1913 as the President's House for Radcliffe College. Originally its brick walls were stuccoed in imitation of stone. An early example of historic preservation occurred here: a Federal-style house (C13) that formerly occupied the site was moved and preserved when this house was built.

C8 83 Brattle Street 1908

NEWHALL & BLEVINS

Although somewhat out of scale with its surroundings, this tall apartment building has an inviting entrance court and is lavishly ornamented with limestone and leaded glass in a neo-Tudor manner. Originally a private apartment house known as Wadsworth Chambers, the building now serves as Radcliffe housing, complementing the facilities of the Radcliffe Graduate Center across the street (1955–1959, Perry, Shaw, Hepburn & Dean).

C9 85 Brattle Street 1847

MICHAEL NORTON, BUILDER

Here is neo-Tudor in its most charming 19th-century form. Norton, a local builder, copied this Gothic cottage from a pattern-book design by New Haven architect Henry Austin. Published in 1847 in the second edition of Chester Hills's *Builder's Guide*, Austin's design was labeled "Villa in the Cottage Style." The buildings of the Episcopal Theological School at Brattle and Mason Streets will be seen at the end of the North of Brattle tour (D57–60). The tour now proceeds left on Ash Street.

C10 90 Brattle Street 1883

H. H. RICHARDSON

A national as well as local architectural landmark, Richardson's Stoughton house is one of the first and finest examples of the domestic American Shingle Style. Weathered shingles envelop the entire exterior surface of the house, now largely hidden behind a high brick wall. Richardson designed 90 Brattle for Mrs. Edwin Stoughton, mother of historian John Fiske, whose own house (D48) was nearby on Berkeley Street. In 1900 Richardson's successor firm, Shepley, Rutan & Coolidge, expanded the house to accommodate Fiske and his extensive library; the additions—mostly to the rear—were sympathetic to Richardson's original design.

C11 9 Ash Street 1941

PHILIP JOHNSON

Johnson built this small house for his own use while he was a student of architecture at Harvard. House and garden are alike surrounded by a ten-foot wall; only the roof projection indicates which part of the property is covered and which open. A glass wall separates the two halves; there are virtually no other windows. Entirely inward turning, the house is the opposite of Johnson's famous glass house of 1949 in New Canaan, Connecticut.

C12 6 Ash Street Place 1848

This Gothic cottage—not so direct a pattern-book copy as 85 Brattle (C9)—is one of the delights of Ash Street Place, a cul-de-sac that ends in a densely wooded garden with a path leading to Fuller Place and Hilliard Street. Back on Ash Street, a fine grouping of well-preserved mid-19th-century houses extends to Mt. Auburn Street and beyond. 12 Ash (on the corner of Ash Street Place) dates from 1846; 14—16 Ash, next door, from 1855. Across the street, 15 Ash (1926, Philip S. Asevy) is the only 20th-century intruder—fortunately, a compatible one.

C13

C13 19 Ash Street 1823
This three-story Federal-style house, built originally on Brattle Street, was moved here in 1858 to make room for Greenleaf House (C7). 19 Ash Street resembles Christ Church Rectory (E4), but there is no documentation for an attribution to builder William Saunders.

C14 153 Mt. Auburn Street 1874
153 Mt. Auburn is the latest in date of four mid-19th-century gabled houses that survive at the intersection of Ash and Mt. Auburn Streets. The house and its former stable have been converted to apartments with admirable respect for original stylistic features. The tour now proceeds back on Ash Street and left on Acacia Street at the Philip Johnson house.

C15 7 Acacia Street 1886
H. C. BURDITT
Stylistically similar to the nearby Stoughton house (C10), 7 Acacia was also enlarged in size not long after it was built. In 1896 Dwight & Chandler added the left-hand circular bay and other rooms to the rear. The front deck and garage wing are 1964 additions.

C16 11 Hawthorn Street 1813
Built originally at the corner of Brattle and Church Streets (site of Sage's Market), this simple Federal-style house was moved here in 1926. Howe, Manning & Almy restored the house and added a garage wing to the rear. Aluminum siding now covers the building but fortunately does not obscure the finely detailed front door frame. The house next door (15 Hawthorn Street, 1896, Ball & Dabney) was also moved, but from just around the corner at 100 Brattle Street (to make room for the Church of Jesus Christ of Latter Day Saints).

C17 94 Brattle Street 17th century; ca. 1746
At 94 Brattle, a 17th-century house was thoroughly expanded and re-modeled in the mid-18th century for Henry Vassall, uncle of John Vassall, Jr., who built 105 Brattle Street (C19). The 19th century brought further changes, including a new raised foundation, removal of roughcast (a form of stucco) from the exterior walls, and a rebuilt east facade with columned porch. Along the Brattle Street frontage is a concrete-block fence that represents an early use of concrete in the city (1870). The Henry Vassall house played a role in the Revolution as the first American Army medical headquarters.

C18 101 Brattle Street 1844
OLIVER HASTINGS, BUILDER
101 Brattle, Oliver Hastings's own house, has something of the spirit of an English Regency villa, with wide corner pilasters, a curved central bay (originally the entrance), ironwork balconies, and a monitor roof. Additions and alterations by a subsequent owner, Episcopal Bishop William Lawrence, do not significantly affect the Brattle Street facade. Now owned by the Episcopal Theological School, the house is sited far back from the street behind a fine granite-and-iron fence.

C19

C19 105 Brattle Street 1759

Built by Jamaican planter John Vassall, Jr., this pilastered Georgian mansion—comparable to Apthorp House (B42) and possibly designed by Peter Harrison—served during the Siege of Boston as George Washington's headquarters. Post-Revolutionary owner Andrew Craigie added side piazzas and extended the house to the rear. Henry Wadsworth Longfellow lived here most of his adult life, from 1837 until his death in 1882. Preserved by the Longfellow Memorial Association, the house is open to the public daily; original woodwork survives along with the poet's furniture. The estate's extensive grounds included land across Brattle Street as far as the river.

C20 Longfellow Park 1883

Longfellow Park maintains a connection between the Vassall-Craigie-Longfellow house and the river. Landscape architect Charles Eliot did the initial layout; architect Henry Bacon and sculptor Daniel Chester French added a memorial to Longfellow in 1914 (on a lower level, beyond the roadway). At one corner of the park is a house (108 Brattle) built in 1870 for the poet's son Ernest, an artist; on the other corner is the Church of Jesus Christ of Latter Day Saints (1955). The Friends Meeting House at 5 Longfellow Park is a 1937 addition by Duguid & Martin to a preexisting house.

C21 113 Brattle Street 1887
ANDREWS & JAQUES

West of the Longfellow house are two houses built after the poet's death for his daughters. 113 Brattle, now the New Preparatory School, was the home of Edith Longfellow Dana. It is a symmetrical, twin-gabled, late Queen Anne design, originally wine-colored.

C22 115 Brattle Street 1887
LONGFELLOW & HARLOW

More thoroughly Colonial Revival than the Dana house next door is this house, built for Annie Longfellow Thorp. It was designed by the poet's nephew, Alexander Wadsworth Longfellow, Jr., who was responsible for much fine Colonial Revival work in the city. Both 113 and 115 Brattle, like their illustrious progenitor at 105, have ample setbacks, making this stretch of Brattle Street one of the most spacious and imposing streetscapes in the city.

C23 112 Brattle Street 1846

Handsomely detailed and in exemplary condition, this Greek Revival house was the first building constructed on the south side of Brattle Street west of the Longfellow property. Next door at 4 Willard Street is an imposing Colonial Revival house of the early 20th century (1904 F. W. A. Machado). Most Willard Street houses are more modest.

C24 8 Willard Street before 1765

This center-chimney house is obviously older than 112 Brattle, but it was built originally on another site. It was moved here in 1908 from 83 Brattle Street to make way for an apartment building (C8). Lois Lilley Howe, a lifelong Cambridge resident and one of the nation's first woman architects, restored and added to the house.

C24

C25

C25 114 Brattle Street 1903
J. W. AMES

Houses such as this one and its neighbors at 118, 120, and 124 Brattle Street, all by the same architect, make clear that Brattle Street has more Colonial Revival architecture than true Colonial. Most of it, as here, is of high quality. This 1903 design makes a good comparison with 1887 Colonial Revival across the street at 115 Brattle (C22). The two buildings are similar, but this one is more archaeologically correct, more easily mistaken for the real thing; early Colonial Revival, as at 115, was freer.

C26 121 Brattle Street 1843

Built by lexicographer Joseph Worcester, this gable-fronted, wide-pilastered house was once the center of a substantial estate on part of the former Vassall-Craigie holdings. Parts of Craigie and Berkeley Streets (seen on Tour D) were laid out over Worcester land. Several small 20th-century houses have been built next door and behind.

C27 128 Brattle Street 1892
CRAM, WENTWORTH & GOODHUE

This house and its neighbor at 126 Brattle Street (1890, Cram & Wentworth) are among the earliest domestic works by Ralph Adams Cram and his partners. Leaded glass, half-timbering, steeply pitched roofs, and massive chimneys are characteristics of both houses, 128 being the more authoritative design. When the two were built, a house formerly facing Brattle Street was moved around the corner to 7 Brown Street. Further along Brattle Street, numbers 130 and 132 (both dating from 1886) are part of the development of Mercer Circle by Gardiner Greene Hubbard, who was also responsible for Hubbard Park (C34–36).

C28 134–136 Brattle Street 1857
This well-preserved double Italianate house has later side bays that are compatible in style. The houses across Brattle Street at the intersection of Craigie will be covered on the North of Brattle tour (27 and 24 Craigie Street, D41–42).

C29 Holy Trinity Armenian Church 1960
JOHN S. BILZERIAN
This recent church is the only non-residential structure on the western part of Brattle Street. The style is traditional, but the tradition belongs to the history of the Eastern church rather than to the history of the neighborhood. Next door at 145 Brattle Street is a Colonial Revival house (1887, Andrews & Jaques) built on the site of the 18th-century Lechmere house, which was moved up the street (C32). Built for William Brewster, an ornithologist who had a private museum on the property, 145 Brattle now serves as Holy Trinity Rectory.

C30 144 Brattle Street 1915
J. W. AMES
This house and its neighbor, 142 Brattle, exemplify early 20th-century Colonial Revival. The placement of the two houses at right angles to each other, both overlooking the same front lawn, is particularly felicitous.

C31

C31 146 Brattle Street 1939

WILLIAM M. DUGUID

This house consciously evokes the form and details, although not the three-story height, of the Lee-Nichols house (C40). The attached garage wing is a concession to modern times. Two magnificent beech trees in front survive from the Victorian estate of Gardiner Greene Hubbard, whose own house (built 1850) stood here. Next door at 148 Brattle is a pre-World War I stuccoed Colonial (1914, Newhall & Blevins); beyond is a 20th-century holdover of the domestic Shingle Style of the 1880's (150 Brattle, 1908, E. B. Stratton).

C32 149 Brattle Street 1761, 1869

The second floor is all that remains of the Richard Lechmere house, one of Cambridge's important Tory Row mansions. In 1869 the house was jacked up a story and given a Victorian main floor and verandah; in 1886 the original top story was taken off and the building moved here from 145 Brattle. Part of William Brewster's development of the Lechmere estate, Riedesel Avenue at the side of the house was named for Baron von Riedesel, Hessian officer imprisoned in the Lechmere house during the winter of 1778–1779. The north side of Brattle Street from here west to the Fayerweather house (C50) is part of the Fayerweather-Lee Historic District.

C33 153 Brattle Street 1803

The Thomas Lee house is a conservative Late Georgian design, more akin to pre-Revolutionary houses than to contemporary Federal work by Bulfinch and others in Boston or Salem. Built for the nephew of Judge Joseph Lee of 159 Brattle (C40), it preserves the spacious siting of 18th-century Tory Row. The fences and landscaping are 20th-century work by landscape architect Fletcher Steele.

C34 152 Brattle Street 1887
CABOT & CHANDLER
This is one of the original houses of
Hubbard Park, a picturesque, romantically landscaped suburban development on the estate of Gardiner Greene
Hubbard. The quadrant-shaped
projecting porch on the far side of the
house once followed the line of a
circular driveway. Although realigned
and paved, the Hubbard Park road still
evokes the feeling of the original
winding carriageway.

C35 20 Hubbard Park 1892
LONGFELLOW, ALDEN & HARLOW
This house and 14 Hubbard Park (to
the left) were both designed in 1892 by
Longfellow, Alden & Harlow, whose
earlier Colonial Revival work included
115 Brattle Street (C22). The houses
of Hubbard Park were originally set on
landscaped grounds without fencing
or other visible separation between
lots. The private tennis court between
14 and 20 Hubbard Park attests to the
development's amenities.

C36 26 Hubbard Park 1894
F. R. ALLEN
The road ends in a cul-de-sac, but one
can continue walking on a path
between this half-timbered neo-Tudor
house and 32 Hubbard Park (1889), to
the right. Facing the path near its
intersection with Lowell Street is 28
Hubbard Park, a 1913 Colonial by
J. W. Ames that represents a second
stage of Hubbard Park development.

C37

C37 7 Lowell Street 1850
MELVIN & YOUNG
Moved back from its original Brattle Street location and somewhat obscured by additions, this cupolaed house was built in the same year and by the same architects as the demolished Hubbard house. The original stable survives behind an enormous beech tree.

C38 157 Brattle Street 1895
WILLIAM G. RANTOUL
Stylistically, this massive neo-Tudor house looks backward to English Queen Anne and forward to 20th-century "English" houses in American suburbs. The interior has been completely remodeled, but the exterior survives intact.

C39 158 Brattle Street 1884
7 Lowell Street (C37) was moved back to make room for this house and its neighbor at 160 Brattle, built the same year. The latter, originally painted in lighter colors, is an informal Queen Anne house with gambrel roof and some Colonial detail. 158 Brattle was the city's first symmetrical Colonial Revival house; its unclassical bow front is the principal indication of its early date. The colors are appropriate and probably original.

C40 159 Brattle Street 1685–1689; ca. 1760

The Lee-Nichols house is the oldest house on this part of Brattle Street and one of the oldest in the city. Its massive central chimney, low-studded rooms, and roughcast left end give evidence of its early beginnings. Built in the 1680's, the house was remodeled to its present three-story form around 1760 by Judge Joseph Lee. Owned by the Cambridge Historical Society, the Lee-Nichols house is open to the public Thursday afternoons. The interior contains 18th-century paneling and some 20th-century restoration work by architect Joseph Everett Chandler.

C41 4 Kennedy Road 1966
DECK ASSOCIATES, INC.

Built into the slope of the hill and landscaped in a naturalistic manner, this Deck House is the most recent addition to Kennedy Road, originally a driveway to the rear of the Frank A. Kennedy house on Highland Street (site of 48 Highland, D28). A remodeled Kennedy gardener's house survives to the right, its tall gabled end contrasting with the low-slung lines of its new neighbor. Allen Jackson designed 15 Kennedy Road, a heavily stuccoed and half-timbered house built in 1932 in much the same style as Jackson's own house of three decades earlier (202 Brattle Street, D7).

C42 11 Kennedy Road 1900
CRAM, GOODHUE & FERGUSON

Underneath modern alterations is one of Ralph Adams Cram's shingled, gabled, half-timbered, neo-Tudor designs (compare 128 Brattle, C27). In front, numbered 161 Brattle, is a 1939 Colonial by Allen Jackson.

C43

C43 163 Brattle Street 1810
Extensive later additions, particularly to the rear, have obscured much of the original character of this house, built for John Appleton on a portion of the former Judge Lee estate (C40). The front part of the house, with its hip roof and its four-window street facade, is the most unchanged.

C44 165 Brattle Street 1873
Built for John Bartlett, Harvard Square bookseller remembered for his *Familiar Quotations*, this Stick Style mansard has its original stable in the rear. The entrance porch is later in date.

C45 168 Brattle Street 1888
ARTHUR LITTLE

This unusual house is Colonial Revival in detail but irregular and unclassical in its massing. The rear facade is more symmetrical. One reason this house appears so strange from the street is that it was oriented with its principal rooms facing south and west over extensive grounds rather than north toward Brattle Street.

C46 170 Brattle Street 1852
OLIVER HASTINGS, BUILDER
The monitor roof on this wide-pilastered house, moved here by the Episcopal Theological School in 1965, recalls a similar feature on Oliver Hastings's own house (C18). On its original site, the front of the house faced Phillips Place and the left side faced Mason Street (the more traveled road); in that position, the service ell to the right (which originally had a one-story front porch) was a less dominant part of the composition than it is today at the corner of Channing Street.

C47 167 Brattle Street 1883
HENRY VAN BRUNT
Architect Van Brunt's own house is typically Queen Anne in its many gables, varied surface treatment, turned porch posts, and irregular fenestration. A luxuriant clinging wisteria vine adds to the romantic effect. Land for this house and those on Channing Place was part of the Fayerweather-Wells estate until the 1880's.

C48 6 Channing Place 1894
LONGFELLOW, ALDEN & HARLOW
This Shingle Style house retains much of its original character, enhanced by the weathered quality of the wooden shingles and the complementary dark green color of the trim. The left front portion of the house is a 1911 addition by one of the original architects, Alexander Wadsworth Longfellow, Jr.

C49

C49 3 Channing Place 1893
SHAW & HUNNEWELL

This large, white, bow-fronted Colonial Revival house differs both from its dark-shingled contemporary at number 6 (C48) and from the stuccoed house across at 2 Channing Place (1922). It is more in keeping with the authentic Colonial mansion (C50) behind which it was built.

C50 175 Brattle Street ca. 1764

Behind a historically accurate 20th-century fence stands one of Cambridge's important Tory Row mansions. Built probably for Jamaican planter George Ruggles, the house was owned during the Revolution by patriot Thomas Fayerweather, who allowed it to be used as a hospital after the Battle of Bunker Hill. 19th-century owner William Wells operated a boys' school here, attended by such pupils as Thomas Wentworth Higginson, James Russell Lowell, and William Wetmore Story. A squash court and garage on the property (1915, Coolidge & Carlson) are now a separate dwelling numbered 177 Brattle.

C51 182 Brattle Street 1895
WILLIAM R. EMERSON

Marking the point where the old highway to Watertown turned (the final section of Brattle Street was not opened until 1812), this shingled house typifies a majority of the late 19th-century houses in the Elmwood Avenue-Traill Street vicinity. The tour route follows the old highway route and proceeds left on Elmwood Avenue. Part of the remainder of Brattle Street (as well as Fayerweather Street, to the right) is included on Tour D.

C52 26 Elmwood Avenue 1899
CRAM, GOODHUE & FERGUSON
A Colonial Revival house by architects better known for their medieval designs (compare 128 Brattle Street, C27, 11 Kennedy Road, C42, and the monastery on Memorial Drive, O21). Perhaps the setting across from Elmwood (C54) helped determine the stylistic choice.

C53 30 Elmwood Avenue ca. 1750
One of the few remaining gambrel-roofed houses in the city, this simple 18th-century farmhouse was moved here in 1965 from Russell Street in North Cambridge, where it was threatened with demolition for a nursing home. The rear lean-to was added when the house was restored, but otherwise the basic structure is original. The sponsor of this preservation project was the Cambridge Heritage Trust, a private nonprofit charitable organization. Known as the Watson house, the building exemplifies on a modest scale the same style and period as its imposing neighbor across Elmwood Avenue.

C54 33 Elmwood Avenue 1767
This three-story Georgian mansion, built by Loyalist Thomas Oliver, was owned after the Revolution by Elbridge Gerry, signer of the Declaration of Independence and the man from whose name the word "gerrymander" was coined. During the 19th century this was the Lowell estate—birthplace and lifelong home of poet James Russell Lowell. Preserved in spacious grounds, Elmwood is now the official residence of the dean of the Harvard faculty. On Mt. Auburn Street, busses are available to Harvard Square; nearby on Larch Road is the starting point of Tour D, a walking route back to the Square.

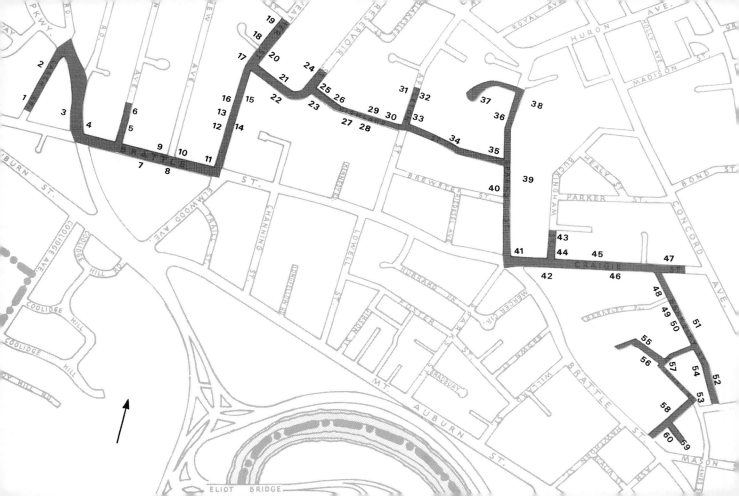

Tour D North of Brattle

Streets to the north of Brattle Street contain as rich an architectural heritage as Tory Row itself, excepting only pre-Revolutionary examples. The environment can be even more pleasant for walking, because there is less traffic than on Brattle Street. This tour follows a route roughly parallel to that of Tour C, in the opposite direction, so that the two tours may be taken in conjunction. Starting at The Larches (just a short walk from Elmwood or from a Mt. Auburn Street bus stop), Tour D heads back toward Harvard Square along the northern fringes of Brattle Street, intersecting Tour C at a couple of places and ending at Brattle and Mason Streets, a few blocks from the Square. Nearly all buildings on the tour are single-family houses, principally from the second half of the 19th century or the beginning of the 20th. There is also a significant number of modern houses, mostly built on sites where large 19th-century houses formerly stood. Tour D has a high proportion of architects' own houses—no less than ten percent of the sixty buildings illustrated. Development along the tour route occurred at different times, under many different auspices, and with a variety of stylistic results, but during the whole period this was the best residential section of Cambridge; so the quality is high. Buildings of two educational institutions—Buckingham School (D38, 45) and the Episcopal Theological School (D57–60)—are included as well as private houses.

D1

D1 22 Larch Road 1808
Built facing south toward what was to become the western end of Brattle Street, The Larches was the summer home of Salem merchant William Gray, whose descendants residing here included lawyer John Chipman Gray. When on its original site, the house had an earlier dwelling—now next door at 36 Larch Road—attached as a service ell. In 1915 the extensive surrounding grounds were subdivided into the Larchwood development, and the Gray house and its ell were moved to their present locations. Alterations were made to both buildings by architect Alexander Wadsworth Longfellow, Jr.

D2 40 Larch Road 1927
HAROLD B. SMILIE
Although not typical in style of the Larchwood development (most of which was "Colonial"), this tile-roofed, stucco-walled, Mediterranean-inspired house shows the revival spirit that characterized early 20th-century Cambridge architecture. More representative of Larchwood is the house next door at 50 Fresh Pond Parkway (1925, J. D. Leland).

D3 36 Fresh Pond Parkway 1910
CHARLES R. GRECO
Architect Greco's own house has a variety of stylistic influences— Colonial, medieval, English, Italian—that are less important than the total effect, which is a style all its own. Features such as arbors, trellises, garden gates, even a detached garage, are carefully integrated into the total design. Stucco (here over terra-cotta blocks) is so appropriate a wall covering that one could imagine no other. This house is a high point of the Stucco Style in Cambridge, by a local architect whose larger buildings are found in several parts of the city (Taylor Square Fire Station, E48; Cambridge High and Latin School, G11; Central Square Post Office, H6; Third District Court, J13).

D4 17 Fresh Pond Parkway 1838

Hidden behind a serpentine brick wall is a much remodeled 19th-century farmhouse built by the Wyeth family. The frame dwelling originally had two bow-fronted bays under a one-story front porch, as on the Nichols house (C5) or 29 Follen Street (E18). In 1909 a substantial ell and a separate stable were added for retired Harvard President Charles W. Eliot (Hartley Dennett, architect). In 1927 Joseph Everett Chandler completely remodeled the house for new owners, adding the brick end toward Fresh Pond Parkway and transforming the house into what is virtually indistinguishable from a 1920's Colonial.

D5 23 Lexington Avenue 1954
CARL KOCH & ASSOCIATES

This Techbuilt house represents a successful prefabricated type that was developed in Cambridge by architect Koch, who long had his offices in the Read house (C4). 23 Lexington Avenue consists of two sections connected by a glassed-in corridor. The lot's natural landscaping provides a taste of the country on this built-up street.

D6 33 Lexington Avenue 1900
JOHN A. HASTY

Although its name commemorates the neighborhood poet (C54), the Lowell is quite out of tune with its surroundings. Still, this elaborately porched and pilastered three-decker has a certain panache, not surprising in the work of an architect like Hasty (compare 367 Harvard Street, G17).

D7

D7 202 Brattle Street 1903
ALLEN W. JACKSON

Jackson was a local Revival architect especially competent in stucco and neo-Tudor designs (compare 48 Highland Street, D28). Since this was his own house, it may be thought to sum up his taste in domestic architecture at the time. An innovation at 202 Brattle Street is the integration of a garage into the main body of the house, quite forward-looking for 1903.

D8 194 Brattle Street 1917
J. W. AMES

Ames was a specialist in 20th-century Colonials that are often mistaken for the real thing by Brattle Street neophytes (compare 114 and 144 Brattle Street, C25 and C30). The distinctive feature of this house, built for artist Felix Schmitt, is the third-story studio window; the entire top floor was originally one huge space. Despite the apparently derivative character of Ames's houses, they are generally ingenious and unstereotyped in their interior planning.

D9 199 Brattle Street 1966
HUGH STUBBINS

Architect Stubbins's own house, the newest on Brattle Street, was built in the front yard of 12 Lake View Avenue (1846). The same vertical boarding covers both the house and the fence around the property. Behind the brick wall along Lake View Avenue lies a swimming pool, completely hidden from view. Lake View is a pleasant street of mostly 19th-century houses, worth returning to sometime for a non-Guided walk.

D10 195 Brattle Street 1895
H. LANGFORD WARREN

Built for Shakespearean scholar George
Pierce Baker, this house is appropriately Elizabethan in inspiration. The
tall chimneys, now slightly leaning,
are especially intriguing. Architect
Warren here used stucco on the ground
story; by the time he built his own
house at 6 Garden Terrace in 1904
(E42), he did not hesitate to cover the
entire building in stucco.

D11 183 Brattle Street 1893
W. Y. PETERS

A dignified, symmetrical Colonial
Revival design by the architect of the
Porcellian Club (B52). Around the
corner at 5 Fayerweather Street is a
simpler house of the same period
(1894, C. Herbert McClare). Across
Fayerweather, with a large front yard
facing Brattle, 4 Fayerweather (1941
David Barnes) occupies the site of
another late 19th-century house.

D12 11 Fayerweather Street 1850

Like 12 Lake View Avenue, in the front
yard of which the Stubbins house (D9)
was built, this mid-19th-century house
once had grounds extending to Brattle
Street. A front piazza still faces in that
direction. Additions and remodelings
(such as the garage wing) have been
accomplished very much in the original
style, which was post-Greek Revival
going Italianate. Across the street, the
brick Colonial reproduction at number
10 is by William M. Duguid (1936); its
clapboarded, gambrel-roofed neighbor
at number 16 is by Andrews, Jaques &
Rantoul (1892).

D13

D13 21 Fayerweather Street 1893
LONGFELLOW, ALDEN & HARLOW

This gambrel-ended mansion is oriented in the same way as 11 Fayerweather Street, with a broad south-facing porch. 15 Fayerweather (1916, Howe & Manning) was built on part of its yard.

D14 22 Fayerweather Street 1898
H. D. HALL

Obviously inspired by nearby Elmwood (C54), this three-story Colonial Revival house has a frontispiece almost identical to that of the Lowell house.

D15 28 Fayerweather Street 1882
STURGIS & BRIGHAM

22 Fayerweather Street is not a surprising design for 1898, but 28 Fayerweather is remarkably Colonial for 1882. Earlier than McKim, Mead & White's Appleton or Taylor houses, this Sturgis & Brigham design, built for A. A. Carey, may well be the first fully developed Colonial Revival house in the country. Despite a certain asymmetry, the house is unabashedly Georgian in its detailing: gambrel roof, Palladian stair window, broken-scroll pediment—all are hallmarks of the style.

D16 27 Fayerweather Street 1896
T. F. WALSH
This early work by Timothy Walsh of
Maginnis & Walsh is comparable to
Ralph Cram's contemporary houses
(128 Brattle Street, C27; 11 Kennedy
Road, C42) in being a shingled neo-
Tudor type. The less said about the
remodeling of 31 Fayerweather, next
door, the better. It was originally a fine
center-gable mansard-roofed house
built in 1863.

D17 37 Fayerweather Street 1901
WARREN, SMITH & BISCOE
Another house sited with its main
facade facing the side yard. Beyond,
Lincoln Lane is a 1920's cul-de-sac
where a single 19th-century house
formerly stood.

D18 45 Fayerweather Street 1940
WALTER BOGNER
Composed with the clarity of the
International Style, this house has a
warmer quality than others of its period
(such as 4 Buckingham Street, D43)
because of the mellow old brick of
which it is built. The brick came from a
house in Boston's Back Bay; the architect was a member of the Harvard
architecture faculty. In the Fayerweather Street tradition, the living
areas of the house are oriented south.

D19

D19 55 Fayerweather Street 1905
RICHARD ARNOLD FISHER

One of the city's best examples of pre-World War I domestic architecture, this brick house is Georgian Revival in style but thoroughly modern (for its period) in plan and orientation. It backs up to Gurney Street on the north, allowing an extensive south-facing garden. Across Gurney Street is a white frame Federal Revival house of the same period (59 Fayerweather Street, 1906, Winslow & Bigelow). At 48 Fayerweather Street is a three-story stuccoed house (1904, Hartley Dennett) built for the same A. A. Carey who had commissioned 28 Fayerweather (D15) twenty-two years earlier.

D20 46 Fayerweather Street 1968
GEOMETRICS, INC. (PETER FLOYD)

This large new house with dramatic shed roofs, illustrated here while under construction, replaces a columned Colonial Revival mansion of the first decade of the 20th century. Some of the stone foundations of the former house are being used for the gardens of this one.

D21 11 Reservoir Street 1965
KENNETH REDMOND

Architect Redmond's own house, covered in natural clapboards, takes advantage of garden views in several directions, particularly across the expansive front lawn of 25 Reservoir (D24).

D22 12 Reservoir Street 1877
WARE & VAN BRUNT

Hard to see from the street, this house is oriented toward its sloping side yard. Turned porch columns and red brick trimmed with black are characteristic of both the period and the architects. So is the steeply pitched slate roof (no longer a mansard) capped by a balustrade (compare 10 Follen Street, E21).

D23 64 Highland Street 1963
F. F. BRUCK

All the new houses in this vicinity except 11 Reservoir Street replace earlier buildings. This one replaced the first house on Highland Street, a Gothic Revival structure of 1860. The crisp, clean lines of 64 Highland are emphasized by the hardness of the purple-gray brick, which creates quite a different effect from the warmth of the red brick at 45 Fayerweather (D18), a house similar in style but twenty-three years earlier in date. The south side of 64 Highland opens through walls of glass to a private rear yard.

D24 25 Reservoir Street 1872
STURGIS & BRIGHAM

Originally entered from a carriage drive on the north, this house was given its present south-facing entrance (with broken-scroll-pediment door frame) in the first decade of the 20th century (Lois Lilley Howe, architect). The rest of the house remains substantially as Sturgis & Brigham designed it in 1872. Stick Style detailing articulates the facades, particularly in a band between the stories. Although the roof is a gambrel, the house is not consciously "Colonial" like Sturgis & Brigham's 28 Fayerweather (D15), built a decade later.

D25 26 Reservoir Street 1955
F. S. COOLIDGE

Reservoir Street was named for a city reservoir that stood on this corner during the 19th century. In 1901 the reservoir lot became the site of a large Colonial Revival house and stable. The shingled stable still exists at 40 Reservoir Street, set back from the street behind a stone wall that was part of the reservoir's retaining wall. The 1901 mansion has been replaced by three modern houses—30 Reservoir (1954), 61 Highland (1958, D26), and this house (1955). Designed by a California architect, 26 Reservoir has low-sloping roofs and natural siding that blend well with the landscape.

D26 61 Highland Street 1958
GEOMETRICS, INC. (WILLIAM WAINWRIGHT)

Organized around an open central court, architect Wainwright's own house has a zig-zag canopy roof over the main living areas and full-height exterior blinds that slide across the bedroom windows in front. Only pedestrians enter from Highland Street; cars take a driveway leading in from Reservoir Street.

D27 54 Highland Street 1886
CHAMBERLIN & WHIDDEN

This distinguished brick house is another of the neighborhood's early Colonial Revival designs (compare 28 Fayerweather Street, D15). Indicative of its 1880's date is the off-center Palladian stair window; uncharacteristic of the decade is the Ionic columns-in-antis entrance porch, which one might think had been added in the early 20th century, except that it appears in an architects' sketch published in 1887. The ground slopes off behind, allowing a full three-story rear elevation. The kitchen, originally in the basement, is now on the main floor in an unobtrusive wing added to the left in 1932.

D28 48 Highland Street 1927
ALLEN W. JACKSON

This "English" house by Allen Jackson stands on the site of an 1863 mansard long occupied by Frank A. Kennedy, Cambridgeport cracker manufacturer (see 430–442 Massachusetts Avenue, H44). The Kennedy name is remembered in Kennedy Road (C41–42), which runs off Brattle Street directly behind this house.

D29 45 Highland Street 1872

This rambling frame house of the seventies, Stick Style if any style, has a good jig-saw entrance porch and a brick stable behind. The house next door (51 Highland) was built at the same time but was subsequently stuccoed.

D30 71 Appleton Street 1876

Almost completely obscured by vines, this brick house trimmed with brownstone and black brick is similar to its contemporaries at 12 Reservoir Street (D22) and 70 Sparks Street (D39). It has a south-facing terrace, as do its neighbors up Appleton Street (D31–32).

D 31

D31 89 Appleton Street 1862
A towered Stick Style mansard, beautifully sited on one of the largest and highest lots in Cambridge. This and the house across the street belonged to members of the Read family, collateral descendants of those who occupied the pre-Revolutionary Read house near Harvard Square (C4).

D32 88 Appleton Street 1859
Originally entered on the south facade, this house had a mansard roof, extensive verandahs, and several bay windows (including one where the present front door is). A thorough remodeling by Winslow & Bigelow in 1922 brought the house to its present appearance. Flush boarding scored in imitation of ashlar masonry remains, as does the basic mass of the house below the cornice.

D33 29 Highland Street 1922
Built in the former front yard of 88 Appleton Street, this house is one of the newest on a stretch of Highland Street opened in 1887. Next door at 23 Highland Street is an 1888 Peabody & Stearns house now shorn of its original top story and roof.

D34 17 Highland Street 1888
CABOT & CHANDLER

Quite a contrast to 23 Highland Street is the authenticity of this shingle-covered house by Cabot & Chandler, complete with original stable (out of sight behind). Across the street are two Colonial Revival houses built fifteen years apart—a gray one with columns (18 Highland, 1897, J. W. Beal) and a yellow one (22 Highland, 1912, Bellows & Aldrich). Andrews, Jaques & Rantoul designed the 1891 shingled house at 11 Highland.

D35 1 Highland Street 1894
LONGFELLOW, ALDEN & HARLOW

In entirely original condition is this fine Colonial Revival house by Cambridge's specialists in the style—compare 115 Brattle Street (C22), 20 Hubbard Park (C35), and 21 Fayerweather Street (D13). The garden, which contains a gazebo, was designed by landscape architect Charles Eliot and renewed in 1925 by his nephew Charles W. Eliot 2d. At the corner of Sparks Street, the tour proceeds to the left.

D36 77 Sparks Street 1950
G. W. W. BREWSTER

A sizable 19th-century estate was subdivided after World War II and built up predominantly with modern houses, of which this is one example. The siding is painted a typical 1950's-modern dark red. The stained-clapboard house at 2 Hemlock Road (built, believe it or not, in 1954) is the one anachronism in this development.

D37

D37 5 Hemlock Road 1956
JAMES C. HOPKINS, JR.

Architect Hopkins's own house has a private rear yard screened from the already quite private cul-de-sac of Hemlock Road. Other houses on the circle are number 18 (1948, Andrews, Jones, Biscoe & Goodell) and number 15 (1952, The Architects Collaborative). Trees remain from the former estate, supplemented by additional plantings around the various houses. 9 Hemlock Road (formerly 81 Sparks Street) was built in 1937 (Blodget & Law, architects).

D38 80 Sparks Street 1858

This 1858 mansard was made to look as Georgian as possible through the addition in 1932 of brick veneer, limestone sills and lintels, twelve-over-twelve sash, wide-slatted blinds, and a mansard-suppressing parapet, not to mention brick garden walls and a wrought-iron entrance porch. Architects for the remodeling were Edward Sears Read and Charles Everett. Fortunately, original plasterwork and marble mantels were allowed to remain inside, and a charming original stable survives behind. Used by the Buckingham School, the house has a new rear classroom wing by Ashley, Myer & Associates (1968), incorporating an earlier school wing.

D39 70 Sparks Street 1878
LONGFELLOW & CLARK

Nestled in a hollow far back from the street, this Queen Anne house has a picturesque setting befitting its style. Gables, bays, and porches project from the building's steep-roofed mass, creating patterns of light and shadow; dark colors and clinging vines enhance the romantic effect. The house was built for a son of the family that lived next door at 72 Sparks Street; 72 was moved forward on its lot so that each house would overlook an ample side yard rather than a closely adjoining building.

D40 61–67 Sparks Street 1875

Somewhat incongruous on a street of detached houses, this brick row was the first building erected by John Brewster and his son William in their development of the Lechmere estate; within fifteen years they had built up most of Brewster Street and Riedesel Avenue and had moved and replaced the Lechmere house (C32). Ornamental features of 61–67 Sparks include Nova Scotia sandstone and panels of fancy brickwork; dormers rise above dormers on the high mansard roof. A more recent incongruity is Holy Trinity Armenian Church (C29) at the corner of Brattle Street. The tour proceeds left on Craigie Street.

D41 27 Craigie Street 1853
HENRY GREENOUGH

This villa-like Italianate house was Henry Greenough's last premansard design. Formal and symmetrical, as were all of Greenough's houses, it was built for Professor Arnold Guyot and was long the home of Professor Eben Norton Horsford, noted chemist and Norsophile. A brick stable added by Horsford in 1882 is out of sight behind. Next door at 25 Craigie Street is a wide-pilastered center-gable house built in 1856 (K. W. Baker, builder).

D42 24 Craigie Street 1868
JAMES R. RICHARDS

The Ross house is Cambridge's most imposing mansard mansion, impressively sited at the intersection of Craigie and Brattle Streets. There are three principal facades, each tripartite and formal in the best French Second Empire manner. The house was built for Albion K. P. Welch, who died before occupying it; the Ross family has lived here ever since. Artist Denman Ross added a studio to the ell in 1893. The concrete-block fence around the property is contemporary with the house; it is similar to (but simpler than) the one in front of the Henry Vassall house (C17).

D43

D43 4 Buckingham Street 1937
CARL KOCH AND EDWARD D. STONE
An early work by two important
Cambridge-trained architects,
this concrete-block house helped to
introduce International Style principles
to the city. A wall of random blocks of
slate provides privacy to the front
garden and offsets the building's severe
lines.

D44 23 Craigie Street 1855
OLIVER HASTINGS, BUILDER
Oliver Hastings was a builder who
ran the gamut of styles in his time—
compare (in chronological order) 69
Dunster Street (B17), 38 Kirkland
Street (A49), and 101 Brattle Street
(C18). Here he worked in the Italianate
style, with round-headed windows,
heavy brackets, balconies, and balus-
trades. The mansard roof may or may
not be a later addition; there is some
difference of opinion.

D45 Buckingham School Primary
Building 1967
ASHLEY, MYER & ASSOCIATES
Buckingham School's new building on
19th-century Craigie Street is com-
fortably in scale with its neighbors.
Stucco is used as an exterior finish, in
conjunction with columns and lower
walls of raw concrete. Next door at
15 Craigie Street is an 1870 mansard
house with balustraded terrace to the
side.

D46 14 Craigie Street 1869
This mansard cottage has undergone a
few changes (such as the addition of a
sleeping porch in 1912), but it retains
much of its original style and charm. It
is the fifth in a series of Craigie Street
mansards (including the Ross house)
built within a few years of each other.
Across at the end of Craigie Circle is a
three-story Colonial Revival house
(1910, Albert G. Hall). This and the
Craigie Circle apartments (1917–1920,
Hamilton Harlow) replace an 1855
mansard.

D47 3 Craigie Street 1855
ISAAC CUTLER, BUILDER
This simple, unbracketed Italianate
house may well have taken its cue
from Henry Greenough's more imposing Guyot house down the street
(D41). The apartment building to the
right (1 Craigie Street, 1925) is called
the Dean Howells because William
Dean Howells lived around the corner
at 37 Concord Avenue (a house built
for him in 1872). Opposite the end of
Craigie Street is an apartment building
by Hugh Stubbins & Associates (29
Concord Avenue, 1959). The tour now
proceeds along Berkeley Street.

D48 22 Berkeley Street 1877
GRIFFITH THOMAS
Historian John Fiske took great interest
in the design of this house for himself,
specifying such features as a large
book-lined library and a conservatory
off the dining room—both features
that he introduced into his mother's
house at 90 Brattle Street (C10) when
he was preparing to move there in
1900. Compared to Richardson's
design for Mrs. Stoughton, the Fiske
house is remarkably conservative.
In fact, it hardly differs (in mass if not in
detail) from its neighbor of two decades
earlier across Berkeley Place (D49).

D49

D49 20 Berkeley Street 1856
The concave mansard roof of this house is partly concealed by a deep soffit supported by paired brackets. Except for the mansard, the architectural features of 20 Berkeley Street resemble those of the three gable-roofed Italianate houses across the street (23, 21, and 19 Berkeley, all built in 1854).

D50 16 Berkeley Street 1905
HARTLEY DENNETT
This distinguished example of the early 20th-century Stucco Style fits in well with its 19th-century neighbors. Next door at 12 Berkeley Street is an 1881 house with later stucco covering.

D51 15 Berkeley Street 1863
Cambridge's most imposing Italian villa, complete with asymmetrical tower and overhanging bracketed eaves, is hidden by later brown shingles and tall evergreens. Next door to the left, 17 Berkeley Street was once attached to 15 when the latter served as a school; it was detached and made into a house in the early 20th century. Next door to the right, 13 Berkeley is a late shingle-covered Queen Anne house (1898, Dwight & Chandler); beyond, 11 Berkeley is an 1886 design by William R. Emerson.

D52 5 Berkeley Street 1852
CALVIN RYDER

More typical of the city's Italianate houses than 15 Berkeley is this T-shaped design by Calvin Ryder. Its raking cornice, porches, and bays are heavily bracketed; on the facade, round-headed windows are combined with rectangular ones. One-story porches fill the angles of the T. At 3 and 1 Berkeley are two other houses of the period (1856 and 1852, respectively), the latter extensively remodeled to its present three-story height in 1906 (Charles K. Cummings, architect).

D53 4 Berkeley Street 1851

Handsomely sited, this first house on Berkeley Street was built for Richard Henry Dana, Jr., and now serves as the Dean's Residence for the Episcopal Theological School. T-shaped in plan like 5 Berkeley, it established the Italianate mode that dominates the street. The left porch is later 19th-century.

D54 6 Berkeley Street 1853
MOSES AND JEDEDIAH RICKER, BUILDERS

Also T-shaped in plan, this well-preserved Italianate house looks L-shaped from the street but has a similar projecting wing and arcaded porch on the rear. Beyond 8 Berkeley Street (1859, Oliver Hastings, with later additions), follow a driveway left to St. John's Road, a residential compound recently developed by the Episcopal Theological School.

D55

D55 13, 11, and 9 St. John's Road 1820, 1834, 1845

Moved here by the Episcopal Theological School, these houses represent three decades of 19th-century domestic architecture and illustrate the transition from the Federal to the Greek Revival styles. From left to right, 13 St. John's Road is a late Federal center-hall house built in 1820 by Joseph Holmes and moved in 1963 from 14 Appian Way, site of Larsen Hall (E5); 11 and 9 St. John's Road are, respectively, 1834 and 1845 gable-fronted side-hall houses by William Saunders, moved in 1959 from the corner of Brattle and Hilliard Streets, site of Loeb Drama Center (C6).

D56 8 and 10 St. John's Road 1954
HUGH A. STUBBINS, JR.

The beginnings of St. John's Road as a residential cul-de-sac came when the Episcopal Theological School built these two houses. Beyond number 10, at the end of the circle, is the rear of the Longfellow stable (behind 105 Brattle Street, C19). The stuccoed house at 15 St. John's Road (1906, Charles K. Cummings) is another building moved to this land, which formerly was part of the grounds of the Longfellow house.

D57 Winthrop Hall 1892
LONGFELLOW, ALDEN & HARLOW

This puddingstone dormitory follows the medieval inspiration established by Ware & Van Brunt in the original Episcopal Theological School buildings (D58, 60) rather than the Georgian Revival idiom subsequently favored by Longfellow in his work at Harvard (Phillips Brooks House, A8) and Radcliffe (Agassiz House, E9; Bertram Hall, E35). In use of material, although not in massing, the building is comparable to the firm's Abbot house of a few years earlier (E25). Walk beyond Winthrop Hall and through an arched opening between buildings on the right, into the E.T.S. Quadrangle.

D58 E.T.S. Quadrangle 1872–1880
WARE & VAN BRUNT

Forming a quadrangle open to Brattle Street, this range of buildings was designed by Ware & Van Brunt to evoke a Flemish village, with the arcaded central building as the town hall. Viewed from Brattle Street, Lawrence Hall (a dormitory built in 1872 and extended in 1880) is on the left; Reed Hall (offices and classrooms, built 1875) is in the center; and Burnham Hall (originally the refectory, built 1879) is on the right. To Burnham's right, Wright Hall (originally the library) is a 1911 design by Shepley, Rutan & Coolidge.

D59 Sherrill Buliding 1965
CAMPBELL & ALDRICH

This limestone-clad library is the newest building at the Episcopal Theological School. It is viewed here between Washburn Hall (1960, Larsen, Bradley & Hibbard), a dining and recreation center, and Wright Hall (1911), the former library. Serving effectively to wall off the E.T.S. campus from Mason Street, Sherrill is terraced above the surrounding walkways. Dominant feature of the interior is a spacious, stucco-walled central court.

D60 St. John's Chapel 1868
WARE & VAN BRUNT

This stone chapel, a Brattle Street landmark, was Ware & Van Brunt's first building for the Episcopal Theological School. Modeled after English parish churches of the 13th and 14th centuries, the picturesque chapel has an asymmetrical tower with banded stone steeple. Alterations have included a 1930 chancel remodeling by Allen & Collens and a complete interior overhaul, together with a new doorway on the west end, by Campbell, Aldrich & Nulty in 1967. Tour D ends here, just a short walk down Brattle Street to Harvard Square.

Tour E Garden Street

Garden Street takes its name from Harvard's Botanic Garden, established in 1808 at the intersection of what is now Linnaean Street. There has been a road where Garden Street is since the 17th century, although little building occurred along it until the 19th century. The street begins as the southern boundary of Cambridge Common, a survival (along with the Old Burying Ground, E2) from the city's earliest days. The Common originally extended as far as Linnaean Street; it was reduced to approximately its present size in 1724, although it was not fenced in until 1830. Tour E begins at the First Church (Unitarian), just north of Harvard Square, and meanders on and off Garden Street as far as Huron Avenue (a short walk from either the starting point of Tour F or a bus back to Harvard Square). Around the Common are two pre-Revolutionary buildings (Christ Church, E3, and 7 Waterhouse Street, E14), but otherwise the architecture seen on this tour dates from the 19th and 20th centuries. Included are domestic, religious, and institutional buildings—the last largely in two groupings, the Radcliffe Yard near the Common (E6–11) and the Radcliffe Quad between Shepard and Linnaean Streets (E34–38).

E1

E1 First Church, Unitarian 1833
ISAIAH ROGERS

Built for the Unitarian branch of the First Church in Cambridge after the congregation split in 1829, this wooden Gothic Revival church replaced a 1756 meeting house near the present site of Lehman Hall (A71). Although the interior was remodeled in 1928 by architect Allen W. Jackson, the exterior survives much as Isaiah Rogers designed it, except for the absence of finials at the roofline. The stone parish hall at the rear was added in 1901 (J. W. Richards, architect). The church forms an effective southern boundary for the Old Burying Ground (E2).

E2 Old Burying Ground 1635

Revolutionary soldiers, Harvard presidents, and other early Cambridge citizens are buried in this cemetery, which, apart from its historical associations, is an oasis of calm just a few steps from Harvard Square. Entrance to the Burying Ground is just to the right of the Unitarian Church; meandering paths lead past three centuries of gravestones to a gate behind Christ Church (E3).

E3 Christ Church 1760
PETER HARRISON

Facing Cambridge Common is Christ Church, the city's oldest surviving religious structure. Architecturally significant as the work of Newport gentleman-architect Peter Harrison, it is a simple wooden building with arched windows and a Doric frieze. It was lengthened two bays in 1857 but otherwise remains substantially as built. The interior with its classical columns and entablature is more elaborate than the exterior, but without a gallery it seems modest compared to Harrison's King's Chapel in Boston. Christ Church's original parishioners were Tories who fled at the outbreak of the Revolution, during which troops occupied the building.

E4 1 Garden Street 1820
WILLIAM SAUNDERS, BUILDER

Christ Church's rectory was not designed as such, despite the appropri-
ateness of its setting for the purpose.
The three-story, hip-roofed, late
Federal-style house was built by
master builder William Saunders as his
own home, where he lived until his
death in 1861. The houses next door
are later in date: 2 Garden Street (also
by Saunders), 1835; 3 Garden Street,
1851. Across the street, in the Common, rises Cambridge's Civil War
Monument (1869; Cyrus and Darius
Cobb, artists; Thomas W. Silloway,
architect).

E5 Larsen Hall 1965
CAUDILL, ROWLETT & SCOTT

This newcomer to the Cambridge
Common scene is, despite its height,
quite compatible with the red brick
buildings of Radcliffe across Appian
Way. Built for the Harvard Graduate
School of Education, Larsen Hall contains offices, classrooms, and multi-
purpose space, some of it opening onto
a sunken plaza. The white frame house
next door (10 Appian Way, 1855) is—
or will soon be—the only surviving
Appian Way house on its original site.
The romantically named block-long
street was laid out in 1810. Beyond,
toward Brattle Street, will be the school
of Education Library, designed by
Benjamin Thompson & Associates.

E6 Longfellow Hall 1929
PERRY, SHAW & HEPBURN

Built for Radcliffe and now occupied
by the Harvard School of Education,
Longfellow Hall was the first major
building to disrupt the domestic appearance of Appian Way, though
Radcliffe had since its founding in
1879 been quartered in the vicinity.
The architects (who were in charge of
the restoration of Williamsburg, Vir-
ginia) here chose Bulfinch's University
Hall (A4) as their inspiration; the
parallel is better seen on the inner,
Yard side (illustrated) than on the
Appian Way facade. Take the path to
the right of Longfellow Hall, noting
the brick-walled garden that extends
toward the Common.

E7

E7 Byerly Hall 1931
COOLIDGE & CARLSON

Radcliffe's science building has an inordinate number of chimneys, which helped to inspire the upper massing of Larsen Hall. The chimneys serve as vents for the laboratories inside. The design of Byerly follows the precedent set by its earlier neighbors; the specific sources seem to have been Harvard's Hollis and Stoughton Halls (A5–6).

E8 Radcliffe Institute 1907
WINSLOW & BIGELOW

Replaced as Radcliffe's main library by Hilles Library (E37), this building was remodeled in 1966 to accommodate the Schlesinger Library and the Radcliffe Institute. New work includes round-headed roof dormers and glazed gable ends.

E9 Agassiz House 1904
ALEXANDER WADSWORTH LONGFELLOW, JR.

An imposing four-columned facade proclaims Agassiz House as the central building of the original Radcliffe Yard complex. The library, Agassiz House, and the gymnasium—all by different architects—are linked by colonnades in a Jeffersonian manner. Agassiz contains a theater and function rooms.

E10 Radcliffe Gymnasium 1898

McKIM, MEAD & WHITE

Preceding McKim, Mead & White's Harvard Union (A62), the gymnasium was Radcliffe's first red-brick neo-Georgian building. The style endured for half a century at both Harvard and Radcliffe.

E11 Fay House 1806

The core of this structure, substantially rebuilt in 1890 by Longfellow, Alden & Harlow, is an 1806 Federal mansion. Virtually nothing of the original is visible from the Yard, but some curved bays (the lower portions of which were part of the first house) survive on the Garden Street side. At the center of the intersection of Garden and Mason Streets, embedded in the pavement, a bronze plaque marks the site of the Washington Elm, a tree under which (traditionally but not authoritatively) Washington took command of the Continental Army on July 3, 1775.

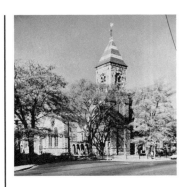

E12 First Church, Congregational 1870

ABEL C. MARTIN

This traprock church trimmed with granite and brownstone originally had a tall stone spire, removed and rebuilt in its present form in 1938 (Allen, Collens & Willis, architects). The weathercock atop the tower roof is considerably older than the church itself, having been made in 1721 for Boston's New Brick Meeting House on Hanover Street. The rear portion of the building is a 1926 parish house addition by W. H. McLean, winner of a competition for the design. The First Church, Congregational, is the orthodox branch of Cambridge's first church; the Unitarian branch has its meeting house in Harvard Square (E1).

E13

E13 1 Waterhouse Street 1916
NEWHALL & BLEVINS

The apartment buildings on the north side of the Common provide, through their height and mass, a good backdrop to the Common's open space. Newhall & Blevins designed the entire grouping of six-story apartments at the Garden Street-Concord Avenue-Waterhouse Street intersection. Courts, bays, and terra-cotta or limestone trim are characteristic features of these structures, built over the years 1915–1926. The Sheraton-Commander Hotel, with its flat facades, cast-stone trim, and imitation Mt. Vernon portico, dates from 1926.

E14 7 Waterhouse Street ca. 1753

This house and Christ Church (E3) are the only surviving buildings (besides Harvard's) that fronted on the Common during the Revolution. At the time, the house was only half its present size. The right-hand two bays were added sometime after 1781, probably during the occupancy of Dr. Benjamin Waterhouse, scientist, Harvard professor, and introducer of smallpox vaccine to the United States. The two-story gabled entry is a 19th-century addition. Next door, on former Waterhouse land, is an 1887 Colonial Revival house (Chamberlin & Whidden, architects), now Red Cross headquarters.

E15 First Church of Christ, Scientist 1923

This Pantheon-type church works well on its trapezoidal site, where it replaces a 19th-century house moved around the corner (44 Follen, E17).

E16 Harvard-Epworth Methodist Church 1891

A. P. CUTTING

Located across Massachusetts Avenue next to Hastings Hall (A17) and not far from Richardson's Austin Hall (A15), this tall-towered church has strong Richardsonian overtones, particularly in its entrance arch and dark-toned masonry. Further up Massachusetts Avenue is a new Law School administration and classroom building by Benjamin Thompson & Associates (compare their Faculty Office Building, A18).

E17 44 Follen Street 1862

Originally located on the site of the Christian Science Church, this brack-eted mansard house was moved in 1923 to its present cramped location, where it accommodates the Law School's Lincoln's Inn Society. The new front door is unfortunate, but otherwise the house (on the outside, at least) is substantially intact.

E18 29 Follen Street 1837

Strategically located where Follen Street turns a sharp corner, this charming house is similar to the Nichols house (C5) in having bowfronted bays under a one-story porch, but its trim is heavier and more Greek Revival in character (befitting the 1837 date). The presence of just one window in each of the curved bays is unusual. Next door is an 1889 gambrel-roofed Colonial Revival by Longfellow, Alden & Harlow.

E19

E19 21 Follen Street 1841
A small, conservative, side-hall house, built at a time when Greek Revival pediment and pilasters would have been expected. Only the door hood is a later 19th-century addition. The house next door, built in 1843, has been considerably modified.

E20 22 Follen Street 1951
CARLETON R. RICHMOND, JR.
A modern house that fits in well on this predominantly 19th-century street. 20 Follen Street, next door, is from the same period (1949, Arthur H. Brooks, Jr.).

E21 10 Follen Street 1875
PEABODY & STEARNS
This imposing Stick Style house, in pristine condition, stands in what was formerly the back garden of the Waterhouse house (E14). 10 Follen has the basic blocklike shape of mansard-roofed houses of the previous decade (compare 44 Follen, E17), but the roof is a high truncated hip rather than a mansard, and the trim (particularly on the elaborate entrance porch) is typical of the seventies (compare 45 Highland Street, D29).

E22 15 Follen Street 1900

WARREN, SMITH & BISCOE

Two houses were built in 1900 on
what had been a single houselot. 15
Follen Street, in front, is by Warren,
Smith & Biscoe; 13 Follen, to the rear,
is by Guy Lowell. One of the charms of
Follen Street is the successful combination of buildings of diverse periods
and styles — unified by their all being
(originally, at least) single-family
houses.

E23 9 Follen Street 1844

Number 9 is one of the earlier Follen
Street houses. Its detailing is robustly
Greek Revival, from entrance porch to
dormers.

E24 5 Follen Street 1853

MOSES AND JEDEDIAH RICKER, BUILDERS

The decade of the 1850's is represented
on Follen Street by this T-shaped,
bracketed Italianate house, comparable to designs on nearby Berkeley
Street (D52–54). Across the street,
the mansard-roofed houses at 6 and 8
Follen were built in 1868 and 1871,
respectively. The white bracketed
house at the corner (9 Concord Avenue) dates from 1855.

E25

E25 Longy School of Music 1889
LONGFELLOW, ALDEN & HARLOW
Built as a private residence for Edwin H. Abbot and now used by the Longy School, 1 Follen Street is one of the most substantial houses in Cambridge, principally because of its granite construction. Around the corner, the Longy School is building a concert hall-library addition designed by Huygens & Tappé. A Roman brick wall surrounds the property, which once extended to Chauncy Street. Before Abbot bought the land, there was a state arsenal here—thus the name Arsenal Square for the intersection of Concord Avenue and Garden Street, with its Spanish-American War statue by Thomas Kitson.

E26 33 Garden Street 1905
CHARLES K. CUMMINGS
Across Chauncy Street from the Continental Hotel (1929) is this symmetrical stuccoed house with central arched loggia—an Italian villa updated for early 20th-century American living. The house next door (39 Garden or 1 Walker) is of the same period (1906, J. H. Wright).

E27 45 Garden Street 1885
This Shingle Style house, enlarged in the 1890's, has recently been re-shingled in an appropriate manner. Opposite, at 44 Garden Street, is an immaculate Colonial Revival design (1894, F. Morton Wakefield).

E28 12 Walker Street 1901
WILLIAM R. EMERSON
This late work by Emerson shows little change from his style of more than a decade earlier (compare 95 Irving Street, A46). Walker Street was laid out and initially developed in the 1870's. Although the architecture is unassuming, the street is particularly pleasant because of the way it turns a corner and extends into several cul-de-sacs.

E29 30 Walker Street 1872
One of a pair of gable-fronted side-hall single houses, illustrating the persistence of that vernacular type.

E30 35–37 Walker Street 1874
GERRITT J. BENNINK & WILLIAM G. DOUGLAS, BUILDERS
One of four identical mansard cottages built for speculation. Except for front porch changes, the four are in remarkably intact condition. The original lower-slope roof slate is all there, and no artificial siding covers the scored flush-boarded facades or the clapboarded sides and rears. Each of the buildings is a double house, as the two sets of front doors indicate.

E31

E31 44 Walker Street 1880
Perhaps the most exaggerated Queen
Anne house in Cambridge, 44 Walker
could have been taken right out of the
pages of a contemporary pattern book.
It contrasts sharply with its conservative next-door neighbor at 42 Walker
(1871). The chimneys have windows
in them, located above fireplaces on
the first floor. At the rear of the lot is a
round-gabled, mansard-roofed stable
that predates the house.

E32 57–59 Walker Street 1871
This full-size mansard double house
with central pavilion over the porch is
an effective focal point where Walker
Street makes a right-angle turn.

E33 68–70 Walker Street 1872
Another double house, this mansard
cottage resembles the four just seen
around the corner but is somewhat
more elaborately ornamented.

E34 Jordan Cooperative Dormitories 1960

CARLETON GRANBERG

These cooperative residences—two buildings, three entries—were Radcliffe's first attempt at modern architecture. Brick neo-Georgian had previously held sway, as seen in the adjacent Radcliffe Quadrangle (E35–36).

E35 Bertram Hall 1901

ALEXANDER WADSWORTH LONGFELLOW- JR.

Bertram Hall at 53 Shepard Street was the first Radcliffe dormitory in this neighborhood. In 1907 the same architect designed Bertram's twin, Grace H. Eliot Hall at 51 Shepard Street (corner of Walker). Both Bertram and Eliot Halls have rear terraces facing the Radcliffe Quadrangle.

E36 Moors Hall 1947

MAGINNIS & WALSH

Moors Hall is the central building of a dormitory complex closing the upper end of Radcliffe's residential quadrangle. Compared to postwar housing efforts at Harvard or M.I.T. (Graduate Center, A20; Baker House, I17), Moors Hall is retardataire in style, but it was meant to complement the earlier Quadrangle buildings and complete the monumental scheme. On the left side of the Quadrangle are Barnard and Briggs Halls (1912, Kilham & Hopkins; 1923, Elwell & Blackell Co.). On the right are Whitman and Cabot Halls (1911, Kilham & Hopkins; 1936, Ames & Dodge).

E37

E37 Hilles Library 1965
HARRISON & ABRAMOVITZ
Different in function and style from its
Radcliffe neighbors, Hilles meets the
college's need for a library near the
dormitories. The building replaces the
old Yard library (E8), built in the days
when Radcliffe was predominantly a
commuter college. Hilles appears
formal and monumental, but formality
breaks down inside into a series of
intimate book alcoves and study
spaces, and monumentality outside is
tempered by sensitive terracing and
planting.

E38 Daniels Hall 1965
HARRISON & ABRAMOVITZ
Daniels Hall is the first unit of a new
Radcliffe dormitory complex by Harrison & Abramovitz, architects of Hilles
Library. Red brick walls recall the older
dormitories, but Georgian stylistic
references have been entirely purged.
Radcliffe now has a House system
modeled on Harvard's; this new residential complex is the first to be designed with the new system in mind.

E39 58 Garden Street 1848
Garden Street once had a number of
important 19th-century mansions;
here is one that has survived. The basic
hip-roofed mass of the house is the
1848 original; the front entrance porch
is a 1901 addition by architects Little &
Browne.

E40 Harvard Observatory 1844–1851
ISAIAH ROGERS

Illustrated here is the original Observatory group, only the central portion of which still exists, surrounded by later, less interesting structures. The Observatory's presence here should nevertheless be noted, since it has long been a Garden Street landmark. Earlier, the slope of Observatory Hill was the site of a summerhouse belonging to the Vassall-Craigie estate (C19).

E41 Botanic Garden Apartments 1949
DES GRANGES & STEFFIAN

Harvard's Botanic Garden was established on this site in 1808 and remained until after World War II. Many of the garden's trees and specimen plants were retained during construction of this university housing project, which includes two-story and three-story apartment buildings along Fernald Drive and single and double houses on Robinson Street (both new streets named after 20th-century Harvard botanists). At 79 Garden Street is Kittredge Hall (1911–1914, William L. Mowll; enlarged 1941, W. H. Andrews). Formerly the Gray Herbarium, Kittredge Hall now serves as offices for the Harvard University Press.

E42 6 Garden Terrace 1904
WARREN, SMITH & BISCOE

Opposite Kittredge Hall lies Garden Terrace, an early 20th-century cul-de-sac. 6 Garden Terrace, a good example of the period's Stucco Style, was H. Langford Warren's own house. Warren was the organizer and first head of the Harvard Department of Architecture.

E43

E43 84 Garden Street 1922
PUTNAM & CHANDLER

84 Garden, built in the 1920's, is Cambridge's grandest "17th century" house. No early Cambridge settler ever had a mansion on this scale.

E44 88 Garden Street 1810
ITHIEL TOWN

Originally located in the Botanic Garden, approximately on the site of Kittredge Hall, this pilastered, balustraded house is a more elaborate example of the Federal style than Cambridge is wont to see. It is the first documented work of architect Ithiel Town, fresh from architectural studies with Asher Benjamin in Boston and soon to achieve fame and fortune in New Haven and New York. Occupied from 1844 to 1888 by botanist Asa Gray, the Garden House is now known as the Asa Gray house. It was moved to its present site in 1910 and restored by architect Allen Cox.

E45 4 Gray Gardens West 1922
HOWE & MANNING

Gray Gardens is a development of the 1920's built on the former Edwin Dresser estate. Most Gray Gardens houses are Georgian in inspiration, such as this one or its neighbor across the street (3 Gray Gardens West, 1926, Putnam & Cox).

E46 20 Gray Gardens West
Here is an authentic Late Georgian
house—probably from the 1790's—on
a cul-de-sac of reproductions. Moved
here from Duxbury in 1930, it was
restored by architect Clarence W.
Brazer.

E47 99 Garden Street 1842
Relic of another era, this Greek Revival
cottage was built for a member of the
Wyeth family, early landowners in the
vicinity. The Wyeth homestead stood
further along Garden Street, approximately where Huron Avenue extends
to the right.

E48 Taylor Square Fire Station 1904
CHARLES R. GRECO
The intersection where this fire station
stands was previously known as Wyeth
Square after the family that built 99
Garden Street (E47). Tour F (Avon
Hill) begins at the end of Huron Ave-
nue, two blocks to the right. An alter-
native route to Raymond Street would
be along Gray Gardens East, compar-
able in style and date to Gray Gardens
West, just seen, but with a modern
house at number 22 (1962, F.
Frederick Bruck). Busses back to
Harvard Square are available at the
intersection of Concord and Huron
Avenues, two blocks to the left.

Tour F Avon Hill

Avon Hill is a residential district between Garden Street and Massachusetts Avenue on either side of Linnaean Street. The hill proper is north of Linnaean, reaching its crest along Washington Avenue. Much of the land in this district belonged to the Cooper-Frost estate, the homestead house of which still exists (F23). Residential development (mostly in the form of single-family houses) occurred in the second half of the 19th century, especially in the years 1870–1900. The area still preserves much of the atmosphere of that era, despite the intrusion of 20th-century apartment buildings along Linnaean Street. There has been a road along the line of Linnaean Street since the 17th century, when Cambridge Common extended that far; the street's name (bestowed in the 19th century because of proximity to the Botanic Garden) comes from the Swedish botanist Carolus Linnaeus. The district's street pattern is rather haphazard because development came at various times under different ownerships; one pleasant result is a large number of block-long streets and cul-de-sacs. Tour F, which connects with the Garden Street tour, begins on Raymond Street opposite Huron Avenue and ends near Porter Square, where transportation is available to Harvard Square and elsewhere.

F 1

F1 79 Raymond Street 1857
Two magnificent beech trees flank the facade of this mid-19th-century mansion, which stands in grounds that are large even by Avon Hill standards. The building's mansard roof has been obscured by a later parapet, but the entrance porch, corner quoins, brackets, and most other details are original. A two-story brick garage building (83 Raymond Street, 1930, Frost & Raymond) replaces a 19th-century frame stable on the rear corner of the lot.

F2 87 Raymond Street 1846
This T-shaped Italianate house, modest by comparison with its neighbor at 79, was the first house on this part of Avon Hill. Built in 1846 and enlarged in 1867, it was the home of Cambridge surveyor William A. Mason.

F3 90 Raymond Street 1896
C. F. WILLARD
90 Raymond Street is a finely detailed Colonial Revival residence in entirely original condition. The same architect four years earlier designed 98 Raymond (on the opposite corner of Bellevue) — a house more Queen Anne in feeling, with corner tower, eyebrow dormer, and overhanging shingled gables. The stable of 98 Raymond is now a separate dwelling numbered 102.

F4 103–105 Raymond Street 1898

E. K. & M. E. BLAIKIE

The back side of Avon Hill is less distinguished architecturally than the top of the hill or the Linnaean Street slope, but there are occasional buildings of interest, such as this three-family structure. Two units face Raymond Street; a third, disfigured by a modern deck, is around the corner at 192 Upland Road. Although 103–105 Raymond Street appears basically symmetrical, there is variety in both plan and elevation. The building is a cut above most contemporary multi-family housing.

F5 20 Bellevue Avenue 1886

KELLY & McKINNON, BUILDERS

Laid out in 1886 on land adjoining 87 Raymond (F2), Bellevue Avenue is a pleasant, quiet street lined with unassuming houses such as this one. The street's greatest charm comes from its cul-de-sacs at either end. 20 Bellevue is a remarkably conservative design for 1886; it could easily have been built thirty years earlier.

F6 48 Bellevue Avenue 1886

This mansard-roofed Queen Anne cottage is perfectly sited on the eastern Bellevue cul-de-sac, next to a more conventional two-story Queen Anne house (45 Bellevue Avenue, 1888). Back on Avon Hill Street is a grouping of double houses of the late 1880's and 1890's, all by different architects.

F7

F7 3 Wyman Street 1955
FRANK J. BARRETT
Striking a different note on the Avon
Hill scene is this relatively recent house,
located on the corner of another of the
district's short dead-end streets.

F8 77 Avon Hill Street 1896
This brown-shingled, vine-covered,
gambrel-roofed "cottage" is Queen
Anne in its irregularity, Colonial in its
detailing, Shingle Style in its informal
feeling.

F9 71 Avon Hill Street 1912
A. L. DARROW
Cambridge has few early 20th-century
bungalows, making this one a welcome sight. It has most of the salient
bungalow features—low-sloping
bracketed eaves, central shed dormer,
enveloping front porch, fieldstone
foundation and chimney.

F10 30 Hillside Avenue 1898
D. W. POWER, BUILDER

In both size and siting, this house is more akin to the mansions of nearby Washington Avenue (F26–28) than to its neighbors along Avon Hill Street. Diamond-paned sash, not normally seen on Colonial Revival houses, are used extensively on 30 Hillside Avenue.

F11 24 Avon Hill Street 1872

Flanking the entrance to Avon Place, another cul-de-sac, are two gabled, bracketed, bay-windowed houses of the early seventies—this one at number 24 and its companion at 32 Avon Hill Street.

F12 Peabody School 1960
HUGH STUBBINS & ASSOCIATES

This modern two-story school serving the Linnaean Street-Avon Hill district replaces a hulking late 19th-century school building on the same site. Brick echoes the predominant material of the neighborhood's apartment buildings; open landscaped corners create a sense of spaciousness. Classrooms are built around a central courtyard, visible through the glass doors of the Linnaean Street entrance.

F13

F13 42–44 Avon Street 1849

Streets and lots south of Linnaean Street were laid out in the 1840's. This well-preserved double house and its neighbors to the right come from the district's first period of development. Paired brackets supporting widely projecting eaves are typical of the late 1840's, when the bracketed style began in Cambridge. The porch deck has been extended toward the street, but otherwise the building appears as it did in the 19th century. An original stable survives behind.

F14 38 Avon Street 1854

Slightly later in date than 42–44 Avon Street, this bracketed single house has its gabled stable attached at the rear. A covered front porch was probably part of the original scheme. A similar house —with quoins instead of simple corner boards—can be found at 32 Avon. Between the two houses is a garden that leads back to an all-but-invisible house of the same period (34 Avon). The tour now returns to Linnaean Street.

F15 41–43 Linnaean Street 1922
HAMILTON HARLOW

41–43 Linnaean Street is a good example of the court-type apartment house, with many bays and projections, generous setback from the street, and attractively landscaped yards and courts. The H-shaped building has a rear court like the one in front. Diagonally across the street is Avon Manor (36–42 Linnaean, 1929, Silverman & Brown), built along the same lines as 41–43, but more frugally. The setback is minimal; facades are flatter; there are no bays; and the central court is constricted. Cast-stone trim, quite noticeable on Avon Manor, appears on most Cambridge apartment buildings of the twenties.

F16 39 Linnaean Street 1870
This side-hall mansard cottage with bracketed, vine-covered side porch picturesquely holds its own against more imposing buildings on the other three corners. The stucco wall covering is not original, but the lower-slope roof slates are. A lacy modern fence encloses the rear yard. The house next door (37 Linnaean Street) was originally a mansard cottage like its neighbors. Built in 1872, it was raised a story in 1893.

F17 33 Linnaean Street 1870
33 Linnaean Street is one of the handsomest, best preserved mansard cottages in the city. Noteworthy features include the balustraded front verandah, the polychrome slate, and the narrow rope molding above the dentil cornices and around the periphery of the mansard.

F18 32 Linnaean Street 1863
Whether Gray Gables was named for its gray color or for its location at the corner of Gray Street is hard to say. Certainly its massive center gable, which repeats the mansard profile, is its most distinctive feature. The building's other details, down to the double doors and granite front steps, are also original and full of character. Next door at 34 Linnaean Street (1891, George Nichols) is a late Queen Anne house with spindle-screen porch.

F18

F19

F19 26 Gray Street 1815

Moved here in 1889 from 1705 Massachusetts Avenue, this house is recognizably earlier than its neighbors. The large chimneys, hipped roof, symmetrical proportions, and fan-lighted entrance are characteristic of Federal architecture of the first quarter of the 19th century. To complete the picture, imagine six-over-six sash in place of the present two-over-two.

F20 31 Gray Street 1893
GEORGE FOGERTY

A finely detailed, towered Queen Anne house that stands head-and-shoulders above its later neighbor at 25–27 Gray Street. Original siding (here, narrow clapboards) makes a great difference on a house like this.

F21 27–31 Linnaean Street 1912
JOHN A. HASTY

This early Linnaean Street apartment building has a row-house rather than a court-type plan, with a round bay at the corner and angular bays flanking the various entrances. Trim is limestone, not cast stone. For Hasty buildings of three previous decades, compare 33 Lexington Avenue (D6), 367 Harvard Street (G17), and 763 Massachusetts Avenue (H7).

F22 25 Linnaean Street 1929
BLACKALL, CLAPP & WHITTEMORE
Stratford Manor has its principal entrances through a court that opens on Washington Avenue. Cast-stone trim, much in evidence on the building, suffers by comparison with limestone, but the material did make possible such elaborate effects as the neo-Georgian pediments here.

F23 21 Linnaean Street ca. 1690
The city's oldest complete house, the Cooper-Frost-Austin house was built in two stages—the right half (which originally had a facade gable) around 1690, the left half around 1720. Structural and stylistic evidence does not bear out the traditional date of 1657. The massive pilastered center chimney, steeply pitched roof, overhanging right gable, and rear lean-to give the house an authentic late 17th-, early 18th-century appearance. Owned by the Society for the Preservation of New England Antiquities, the house is open to the public several times a week. Interior features include exposed framing and huge fireplaces.

F24 35 Bowdoin Street 1812
This modest house of the post-Revolutionary period is, except for its venerable neighbor at 21 Linnaean Street, the oldest house in the vicinity. Originally located on Massachusetts Avenue, the house was moved here in the 1840's, when the district was cut up into lots. Later bays on each side enlarge the small interior spaces. The large side yard adds great amenity to Bowdoin Street, counteracting the bulk of the four-story apartment building at 41 Bowdoin. Coincidentally, the house backs up to another early house that was moved in, 26 Gray Street (F19).

F25

F25 24 Linnaean Street 1876
THOMAS ELSTON, BUILDER
Except for replacement of doors and removal of window blinds, this house and its twin next door have survived in pristine condition. Their spacing is generous for houses that are so narrow and vertical in composition.

F26 26 Washington Avenue 1889
HARTWELL & RICHARDSON
The lower part of Washington Avenue, put through in the late 1880's, was built up with large Queen Anne-Colonial Revival houses, four of the most important by Hartwell & Richardson. This is the most "Colonial" of the four, typical of the free Colonial of the eighties. Note the handsome stable at the rear of the lot. Hartwell & Richardson also designed the 1887 shingled house across the street at number 33, now cut up into apartments and altered at the front porch.

F27 37 Lancaster Street 1887
HARTWELL & RICHARDSON
Facing Lancaster Street at the corner of Washington Avenue are this commodious house and its adjoining stable, both in admirably original condition. The facade of the house is almost symmetrical, yet the dark shingle covering strikes a note of informality. Across the street, 36 Lancaster Street (1886, H. Taylor) is more modest and vernacular than the surrounding mansions. Like 37 Lancaster, it retains its original stable.

F28 49 Washington Avenue 1887
HARTWELL & RICHARDSON
Clapboarded rather than shingled, light rather than dark in color, this Hartwell & Richardson house has more Colonial details than 37 Lancaster Street, although its massing is as irregular as the most stylish Queen Anne.

F29 63 Washington Avenue 1873
The section of Washington Avenue above Hillside Avenue was opened some fifteen years before the lower section. This mansard-roofed house is typical of what was built on the upper part of the hill.

F30 37 Arlington Street 1874
Around the corner from a conventional center-entrance mansard cottage at 78 Washington Avenue is this flamboyant creation of the same period. Its cubical mass broken by the prominent polygonal bay that rises above the roofline to an iron-crested turret, 37 Arlington Street exemplifies the transition from the clarity of the academic mansard style to the asymmetry of the Queen Anne.

F31

F31 81 Washington Avenue 1871
The highest point of land on Avon Hill is crowned by this cupolaed mansard, imposingly set back from the street. Applied wooden ornament is lavishly used, especially on the central pavilion. An 1880's stable survives behind. Originally there was an identical house next door, replaced in 1940 by three incongruous Colonial boxes (85–89 Washington Avenue, Morton B. Howard, builder).

F32 91 Washington Avenue 1941
EDWIN G. JOHNSON
Placed at the back of the lot, this house is refreshingly modern by comparison with its contemporaries at 85–89 Washington Avenue. The stable of the twin to 81 Washington Avenue originally stood here. The lot backs up to 48 Bellevue Avenue (F6).

F33 108 Washington Avenue 1924
KENDALL, TAYLOR & CO.
Something of an anomaly in the neighborhood is this brick "Banker's Tudor" house of the twenties. One would expect to find it in Larchwood or Coolidge Hill rather than on Avon Hill.

F34 114 Washington Avenue 1892
More typical of the neighborhood is
this shingled house with corner tower
and facade gambrel. The latter feature
dominates a contemporary double
house (unfortunately covered with
later siding) opposite the end of
Washington Avenue (129–131 Upland
Road, 1890, C. S. Mooney). The tour
now proceeds left on Upland Road to
an interesting grouping opposite Mt.
Pleasant Street.

F35 146 Upland Road 1873
This gable-roofed side-hall house
retains its original character because
modern alterations have been concentrated at the sides and rear. Elsewhere
on Upland Road, alterations have in
several instances destroyed the character of buildings. Even though 146
Upland Road is just a vernacular development house (compare its near
twin diagonally across at 22 Mt. Pleasant Street), attention to preservation
has made it a neighborhood asset.

F36 144 Upland Road 1957
PAUL RUDOLPH
Architect Rudolph altered a 1913
concrete-block garage into this single-
family residence, distinguished by its
private screened garden off the cul-de-
sac end of Mt. Pleasant Street.

F37

F37 140 Upland Road 1887

Sharing the amenities of the court leading to 144 Upland Road is this asymmetrical Queen Anne house, its construction of brick explained by its having been built for one of the Parry brothers, owners of a prosperous North Cambridge brickyard. Terracotta ornament appears in the pediment of the spindle-screen porch and in the unusual applied roundels around the front door.

F38 115 Upland Road 1890
J. MERRILL BROWN

Except for modern siding, this extravagantly porched and gabled house remains substantially as designed. Its porch columns are original, unlike those on another Brown house around the corner (F39).

F39 9 Walnut Avenue 1887
J. MERRILL BROWN

This earlier Brown design has a lighthouse-like cylindrical balconied tower as its dominant feature. Wrought-iron supports replace the original paired wooden porch columns. This house and 6 Walnut Avenue (F40) across the street were built for brothers.

F40 6 Walnut Avenue 1884–1886
Very much in its original state is this shingled Queen Anne house, complete with octagonal tower, circular porch, and stable. Next door at 4 Walnut Avenue is a cupolaed center-gable house, conservative in style for its 1877 date.

F41 33 Arlington Street 1869
This L-shaped Italianate house with balustraded piazza was the home of John Davis, who was responsible for much real estate development in the vicinity. Originally facing Walnut Avenue, it was moved and stuccoed in 1911, when 2 Walnut Avenue (Ernest N. Boyden, architect) was built.

F42 32 Arlington Street 1872
A tall entrance tower and lacy fretwork in the steeply pitched gables set this house apart from its neighbors and contemporaries.

F43

F43 28 Arlington Street 1876
Almost identical to 30 Arlington Street, this highly ornamented mansard has such period features as bay windows carrying up into the roof. Next door at 26 Arlington Street is a subdued 1869 mansard with later tower and gazebo-like corner porch. Beyond, at 24 Arlington, stands a center-gable house set back from the street; built in 1869, it has a Colonial Revival porch and trim (added in 1898).

F44 22 Arlington Street 1862
The original condition of this simple mansard is refreshing by comparison with some of Arlington Street's much-remodeled houses. Numbers 13 and 11 are especially unfortunate examples of the faults of aluminum siding.

F45 12–14 Arlington Street 1864
This gable-roofed double house is similar to its next-door neighbor at 8–10 Arlington Street, also built in 1864. 12–14 has a slightly later porch and doors; 8–10 suffers from inappropriately wide aluminum siding.

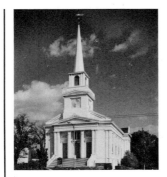

F46 3–9 Arlington Street 1926
BLACKALL, CLAPP & WHITTEMORE
Oxford Court is one of the city's best
examples of the court-oriented neo-
Georgian apartment building. Designed
with stores along Massachusetts
Avenue and an integral parking garage
in back, Oxford Court responds to its
semiurban environment in a way that
few buildings of its period do. Rarely
was off-street parking provided until
required by recent zoning ordinances.
The battlemented apartments across
Arlington Street date from 1904.

**F47 North Avenue Congregational
Church 1845**
ISAAC MELVIN
This handsome Greek Revival structure was built as the Old Cambridge
Baptist Church on the present site of
Littauer Center (A14). The present
congregation bought the building two
decades later, moved it up the avenue,
raised it on a higher foundation to
allow rooms underneath, and subsequently added transepts at the rear.
The steeple has been rebuilt twice,
most recently after a 1964 lightning
fire. Although the present steeple is
inappropriate in style, it provides a
necessary vertical accent.

F48 Sears, Roebuck & Co. 1928
GEORGE C. NIMMONS & CO.
The Avon Hill tour ends at a local landmark that attracts people from further
afield than the neighborhood. Stylistically, the Sears building has overtones
of the "moderne" of the 1920's and
1930's, particularly in the ornament
above the entrance. Across the street is
a bus stop for transportation back to
Harvard Square. Porter Square, with its
post World War II shopping center and
its Boston & Maine train stop, is a
block away to the north. Points of
interest in North Cambridge are included on a driving tour at the end of
the Guide (O29–36).

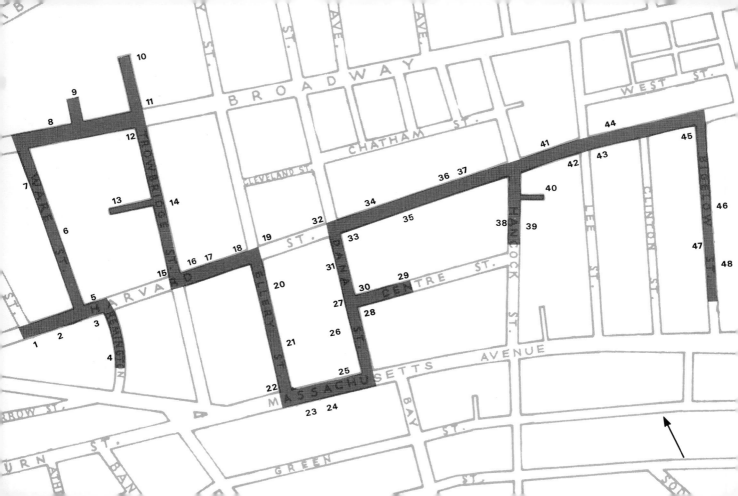

Tour G Dana Hill

Dana Hill was a fashionable residential district in the middle of the last century. First divided into streets and lots in the 1830's and 1840's, (largely on land formerly part of the Francis Dana estate), the district began building up soon afterward. Within a decade there were mansions along the principal thoroughfares (Massachusetts Avenue, Harvard Street, and Broadway)— particularly near the crest of the hill— and more modest houses interspersed among them. Churches and schools were built, but (principally because of restrictions imposed by the Dana family) there was no commerce or industry. Some multifamily housing appeared in the third quarter of the 19th century, as population pressures increased and fashionable districts began opening up elsewhere. Around the turn of the century, apartment house construction began, a trend that has continued to the present day. Few Dana Hill mansions have survived (their large lots were too valuable), but pockets of smaller houses from the district's first period are scattered among later buildings. Although changed and still changing, the district is a pleasant one, offering more of a variety of residential architecture than almost any other part of the city. The tour begins at the Old Cambridge Baptist Church near the intersection of Harvard Street and Massachusetts Avenue and ends at City Hall (Massachusetts Avenue at Bigelow Street), the point of beginning of the Central Square tour.

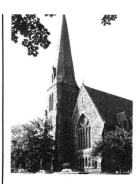

G 1

G1 Old Cambridge Baptist Church 1867
ALEXANDER R. ESTY

This well-preserved stone Gothic church is comparable to, and contemporary with, H. H. Richardson's earliest ecclesiastical works, although Richardson was just at the start of his architectural career, whereas Esty was well along on his. One of Esty's earlier buildings was the Prospect Congregational Church (H16), an example of Romanesque before Richardson. A tall stone spire and patterned slates in the steeply pitched, dormered roof are notable features of the Old Cambridge Baptist Church.

G2 396 Harvard Street 1914
R. CLIPSTON STURGIS

The Elks Home was originally a Harvard clubhouse. Gambrel-roofed neo-Georgian was a predictable architectural choice.

G3 382–392 Harvard Street 1889
RICHARDS & CO.

This multifamily dwelling, more imaginative than most, has a separate entrance for each unit. Most of its original stylistic features—turned porch columns, windows, doors, and variegated siding—have survived, not the case with the remodeled mansards further along Harvard Street. Around the corner at 15 Remington Street is an 1892 three-decker (J. R. & W. P. Richards), also more distinctive than others of its type.

G4 11–13 Remington Street 1846
NATHANIEL U. STICKNEY & SUMNER P. SHEPARD, BUILDERS

This double Greek Revival cottage, built during Dana Hill's first period of development, represents the district's smallest possible housing type. The standard-size Greek Revival house next door (9 Remington Street) is more typical. Across the street is Remington Gables, a 1910 apartment house by Newhall & Blevins.

G5 383 Harvard Street 1893
GEORGE FOGERTY

Ware Hall, now apartments, was originally a private dormitory with communal dining room. A similar but more distinguished Fogerty building is Claverly Hall (B39). Ware Hall is embellished with light-colored brick instead of stone—a cheap imitation that looks like one. Still, the building has more presence and style than Pennypacker Hall on the opposite corner of Ware Street—a 1927 apartment building that now serves as a Harvard freshman dormitory.

G6 14 Ware Street 1933
STURGIS ASSOCIATES

This brick neo-Georgian structure complete with cupola is sometimes mistaken for a Harvard House. Actually, it contains telephone switching apparatus.

G7

G7 23–29 Ware Street 1886
Organized on the row-house principle, with vertically divided living units instead of flats, this towered, mansarded brick block is among the last Cambridge examples of row housing. The emerging type was the "decker" apartment house, such as The Stanstead next door at 19 Ware Street (1887, J. R. & W. P. Richards). The latter building, with its Romanesque entrance arch and patterned brickwork, is considerably more interesting than 20th-century apartments such as The Warren and The Harding across the street (18–20 Ware, 1923, S. S. Eisenberg).

G8 Rindge Technical High School 1932
RALPH HARRINGTON DOANE

Rindge Tech is a sprawling building of white limestone and black metal sash. Although it appears irregular along Broadway, where a rounded auditorium wing projects, its main facade (facing the side of the Public Library) is rigidly symmetrical. Even with few overtly classical references, the building is stylistically akin to its contemporary, the Central Square Post Office (H6). It replaces Rotch & Tilden's Richardsonian Romanesque Manual Training School (1888), one of several gifts to the city from Frederick Hastings Rindge, after whom Rindge Tech was named.

G9 Cambridge Public Library 1888
VAN BRUNT & HOWE

The public library stands at the center of an educational complex inspired and largely donated by F. H. Rindge. Rindge gave the land to the city and paid for construction of the library and Manual Training School (as well as City Hall, H1). The library building is Richardsonian in style, although it contains functional innovations creditable to Van Brunt & Howe—notably the use of book stacks as opposed to an alcove system. Rear additions were made to Van Brunt & Howe's designs in 1894 and 1901; a sharply contrasting 1966 wing is by Shepley, Bulfinch, Richardson & Abbott.

G10 Old Latin School Building 1898

HARTWELL, RICHARDSON & DRIVER

Along a closed-off portion of Trow-bridge Street, facing the public library, stands the yellow-brick Latin School building, now incorporated with Cambridge High and Latin. A similar structure for the English High School (Chamberlin & Austin, 1892) once fronted on Broadway where the main CHLS building (G11) now stands. To the Latin School's left is the red-brick War Memorial Gymnasium and Pool (1955, Richard Shaw), with a band shell facing Library Park.

G11 Cambridge High and Latin School 1939

CHARLES R. GRECO

The main building of Cambridge High and Latin is a pre-World War II structure of red brick and limestone, its style transitional between "traditional" and "modern." Design elements include glass block in the stairwells, a pair of curious, squared-off cupolas, and the watered-down-classical ornament of the thirties. The ornament appears in expected places (such as pillar capitals) but is anything but orthodox in design or execution.

G12 55 Trowbridge Street 1889

JOHN A. HASTY

Back in the residential part of Dana Hill, this Queen Anne house with porch-encircled corner tower survives in substantially original condition, unlike the house next door. Architect Hasty, who did a fair amount of work in the vicinity, lived at 46 Trowbridge Street (opposite Trowbridge Place), an 1892 house of his own design, recently quite disfigured.

G13

G13 4–8 Trowbridge Place 1968
EGON ALI-OGLU
Built of precast structural members and modular wall panels, this new apartment house is important for its innovations in a normally all-too-conservative building field.

G14 42 Trowbridge Street 1842
Surviving in ample grounds complete with stable, this side-hall house of the 1840's gives a good idea of what 19th-century Trowbridge Street was like. Its well-maintained condition is all the more commendable when compared to recently "renovated" 36 Trowbridge Street next door. Across at 37 Trowbridge, a simple 1871 mansard cottage holds out against encroaching apartment-house parking lots. At 33–35 is a gambrel-fronted double house by John Hasty (1892).

G15 371 Harvard Street 1899
WHEELWRIGHT & HAVEN
The ample scale of this Georgian Revival apartment building (one of the first of its kind in Cambridge) can be appreciated by comparing its story heights to those of Crimson Court next door (375 Harvard Street, 1963, John G. Danielson). Good brickwork, limestone trim, and projecting iron balconies (not fire escapes) enhance the carefully studied proportions of the facade.

G16 369 Harvard Street 1877
Conversion to apartments has not ruined the form and style of this imposing brick mansard, set (typically) on a terrace above the street. Only the front porch and some finials and cresting have disappeared.

G17 367 Harvard Street 1895
JOHN A. HASTY
The Templeton was built by 369's owner, who foresaw the apartment-house trend that has continued to the present day on Harvard Street. Architect Hasty here worked in a monumental Roman classical style, complete with giant Ionic pilasters and a boldly projecting copper cornice. For other multifamily dwellings by Hasty, see 33 Lexington Avenue (D6), 27–31 Linnaean Street (F21), and 763 Massachusetts Avenue (H7). The Templeton contains only eight apartments, each extending the length of the building. Appleton Court, next door at 363 Harvard Street, was built in 1907 (C. H. McClare, architect).

G18 357–359 Harvard Street 1867
This double bow-fronted mansard, like 369 Harvard Street, has been converted to apartments in a way that preserves its 19th-century character. Finely polished front doors and an original entrance porch are highlights.

G19

G19 353 Harvard Street 1930
HARLOW & HARLOW
The President represents the last gasp of the style introduced thirty years earlier by 371 Harvard Street (G15). The trim is cast stone instead of limestone, and the total effect is fussier. At least the building takes advantage of its corner location by having the entrance there. The tour now proceeds right on Ellery Street.

G20 20 Ellery Street 1846
Although remodeled more than once, this gable-fronted house retains its Greek Revival corner pilasters and gingerbread bargeboards.

G21 8 Ellery Street ca. 1840
8 Ellery is the best preserved of a group of simple side-hall Greek Revival houses built for developer Isaac Livermore on the mansion-house lot of the Dana estate. A proposed apartment building at 12 Ellery Street jeopardizes the harmonious appearance of these early Dana Hill houses.

G22 1033 Massachusetts Avenue 1968

HUGH STUBBINS & ASSOCIATES

This new six-story office building is a vast improvement over earlier commercial structures in the vicinity—mostly one-story stores. Replacing an 1867 mansard house (recently a convent) and a vacant lot, the building adds mass, solidity, and simplicity of design to a chaotic section of Massachusetts Avenue, besides helping to wall off the residential part of Dana Hill from the commercial strip. Stubbins's own firm will have its offices here.

G23 1010 Massachusetts Avenue 1899

A. H. VINAL

The Cantabrigia is built along the lines of Hasty's Templeton (G17), with wings providing twice as many apartments per floor. The building's six-story height means that an elevator was part of the original scheme. Decorative detail is simpler than on Hasty's building.

G24 1000 Massachusetts Avenue 1857

CALVIN RYDER

Now serving as offices for Cambridge Seven Associates, this mansion with sweeping mansard roof and prominent center gable was originally the home of Henry O. Houghton, who could overlook his Riverside Press (O16) from here. Aluminum siding on the front and asbestos siding on the sides do some injustice to the building, but the entrance porch, window surrounds, and bracketed eaves are all authentic. This was one of the earliest mansard-roofed houses in Cambridge, though the design lacks the sophistication of Henry Greenough's contemporary work (such as 4 Kirkland Place, A50).

G25

G25 991 Massachusetts Avenue 1902

HARRY D. JOLL

More urban in concept and appearance than most early Cambridge apartment buildings, The Dana has offices on the street floor and four stories of bay-windowed flats above. In the mid-19th century, this section of Massachusetts Avenue was one of the city's most impressive residential streets. A columned Greek Revival mansion stood where the Orson Wells Cinema is today; another (replaced by a gas station) stood on the corner of Dana Street.

G26 5 Dana Street ca. 1840

Several older houses survive in this neighborhood amid 20th-century apartment buildings. 5 Dana Street, its charm enhanced by a large front yard, stands approximately on the site of the late 18th-century Dana mansion, which burned in 1839.

G27 7 Dana Street 1841

NATHANIEL VIRGIN, HOUSEWRIGHT

One of the gems of Cambridge architecture, 7 Dana is a charming combination of Greek and Gothic Revival elements. Pointed arches surmount the columned front porch; elaborate ironwork embellishes the second-floor balcony; and scalloped bargeboards project from the steep, flush-boarded gable. An ancient beech tree provides shade on the south.

G28 8 Dana Street 1848
Despite the addition of a nursing-home wing and the loss of embellishments such as balustraded balconies, this T-shaped house remains a lively example of mid-19th-century Italianate. Characteristic details include flush siding scored to resemble masonry, Renaissance window lintels, bracketed eaves and gables, and, surmounting all, a cupola in the guise of a square tower.

G29 19 Centre Street 1842
ISAAC MELVIN & OLIVER WOODS
One of twin houses near the crest of Dana Hill (the other replaced by Burton Halls, G30), 19 Centre Street was architect Melvin's own house. Robustly Greek Revival in detail, it has a T-shaped plan that presages the Italianate (compare 8 Dana Street, G28, or 5 Berkeley Street, D52). A few changes have been made in the porches, but otherwise the house remains substantially as built. A later brick stable with mansard roof is at the rear of the lot.

G30 10 Dana Street 1909
NEWHALL & BLEVINS
The first major apartment building on Dana Hill, Burton Halls crowns its corner site in an imposing manner. Full of bays, gables, turrets, leaded glass, and other neo-Tudor details, it overwhelms its domestic neighbors but has enough style to carry off the affront, unlike later buildings such as 9 Dana (1927, Hamilton Harlow).

G31

G31 11 Dana Street 1870
Although this sizable mansard cottage has suffered some mistreatment, many of its original details survive. The scalloped roof slates in alternating rows of red and gray are particularly appealing.

G32 341–343 Harvard Street 1855
This well-preserved brick double house is a credit to a block that has been victimized by recent apartment-house construction. Noteworthy features include the original doorways, cast-iron second-story balcony, and brick dentil cornice. Across Dana Street at 337 Harvard is an 1887 house (James P. Kelley, architect) that was moved to this spot in 1898. The porch originally had delicate Ionic columns.

G33 342–344 Harvard Street 1857
More up-to-date stylistically than 341–343 Harvard is this double house built just two years later. Single doors framed by sidelights and toplights have given way to double doors topped by segmental-arch transoms; six-over-six sash have given way to two-over-two; and the gable roof has given way to the mansard or "French" roof. Asbestos siding covers what was there originally, but the effect is not unsympathetic.

G34 335 Harvard Street 1850
One of the city's handsomest copper beeches stands in front of this wide-pilastered, monitor-roofed Greek Revival house, the grounds of which originally extended to Dana Street. To the right, on land now occupied by apartment buildings, was another spaciously sited Dana Hill mansion. Behind 335 Harvard is a stable dating from the later 19th century.

G35 338 Harvard Street 1859
Three similarly painted houses on the south side of Harvard Street differ considerably from each other in style. This central one has Gothic Revival elements (such as pointed arches) on its asymmetrical facade; originally there were bargeboards as well. To the right, at 340 Harvard Street, is an 1897 Colonial Revival house by Arthur H. Vinal; to the left, at 336 Harvard, is an 1858 center-gable bracketed house.

G36 325 Harvard Street 1853
This wide-pilastered house terraced high above the street holds its own despite incongruous additions such as fire escapes and dormers. The graceful five-columned side porch and the balustraded second-floor balconies give an idea of the building's original character. The entrance porch and projecting bay window are probably somewhat later.

G37

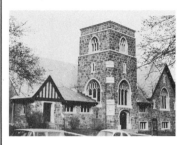

G37 Harvard Street Lutheran Church 1911

NEWHALL & BLEVINS

This puddingstone church with lime-stone trim and stuccoed sides fits remarkably well into its domestic environment. It replaces an 1846 Italian villa, which also had a square tower and asymmetrical gables (though the effect was entirely different). On the corner of Hancock Street is the Stockholm, a four-decker apartment house (1909, W. H. Hunt & Co.). On the other side of Harvard Street is an attractive grouping of modest Greek Revival houses (a double and two singles) from the early 1840's, when the neighborhood began to develop.

G38 123 Hancock Street 1848

Several cottages like this one—each slightly different in plan or ornamentation—were built in the vicinity. 129 Hancock, next door, has been extensively remodeled, but its center-gable stable (now a garage) survives in back. Across the street, 110 Hancock (1839) sports bargeboards and a Gothic Revival gable window. Its contemporary at 104–106 once had a similar latticework porch.

G39 118–126 Hancock Street 1877

This row of five narrow houses has bay windows carrying into the mansard, incised-line decoration, and patterned brickwork—all typical of the seventies.

G40 2–4 Hancock Place 1807
The oldest surviving house on Dana Hill is a historical curiosity. It was put up nearby in order to block the passage of Harvard Street, which local landowners opposed. Opposition House, as it was called, had little effect; Harvard Street went through anyway and was opened in 1808. The modest double house preserves the hip roof and arched-toplight door frames of the early 19th-century Federal style; the doors themselves are of a later date.

G41 307 Harvard Street 1865
Adjacent to a contemporary mansard at 148 Hancock Street, this well-preserved house has a center gable that echoes the mansard profile. This feature and the widely projecting eaves supported by paired brackets are somewhat retardataire for the mid-sixties, but the heavy quality of the ornament is appropriate. Leaded stained glass at the entrance door is later, but the cast-iron fence in front is original.

G42 302–304 Harvard Street 1857
A flat, unornamented facade distinguishes this group of row houses from later examples such as 118–126 Hancock Street (G39). Projecting bracketed eaves are the most noticeable stylistic feature. This row was one of the earliest on Dana Hill; single and double houses were more prevalent in the district. Although neither the color scheme nor the entrance doors are original, the block still makes a handsome contribution to the neighborhood. Particularly pleasant is the setback from the corner.

G43

G43 298 Harvard Street 1888
JOHN A. HASTY

Well maintained as the Jewish Community Center, this towered and gabled house was built for lumber dealer William Wood, whose products were extensively and variously used in its construction. Still Queen Anne in feeling, the house shows little evidence of the Colonial Revival style that was emerging elsewhere in the city (compare 115 Brattle Street, C22). Except for truncation of the tower roof, the exterior is in remarkably original condition; the interior preserves much of the natural varnished woodwork of stairs and mantels, amid modern doors and lighting.

G44 295 Harvard Street 1962
BEDAR & ALPERS

Harvard Towers is one of the most successful new apartment buildings on Harvard Street, besides being the largest. Set back generously from the street and surrounded by a landscaped plaza built over an underground garage, the building provides plenty of light and air to its apartments without overshadowing the neighborhood. Balconies enliven the plane of the facade, which could otherwise be remarkably dull on so large a building; compare the banal exterior of 287 Harvard Street next door.

G45 284 Harvard Street 1887
HARTWELL & RICHARDSON

Built at the same time as several mansions on Washington Avenue (F27–28) by the same architects and builder, this house exhibits similar architectural characteristics, but on a more modest scale. Queen Anne exuberance seems consciously held in check, especially compared with the Jewish Community Center (G43) or with the house on the opposite corner of Bigelow Street (280 Harvard Street, 1886, C. J. Williams).

G46 22 Bigelow Street 1870
Next to a block of twelve narrow row houses (rather haphazardly converted to apartments) stands this imposing symmetrical towered mansard. The reason it seems squeezed onto its lot is that it was moved here when construction of City Hall (H1) pre-empted its original spacious site. Despite peeling paint and a few missing modillion brackets, its condition—down to the brown-and-cream color scheme—is admirably original.

G47 17 Bigelow Street 1873
Bigelow Street was laid out in 1869 and was largely built up within five years. Predominantly mansards, its houses are of two basic plans—symmetrical center-hall types, such as G46, and side-hall types such as this. Artificial siding has been rampant along the street; this house is one of the few with its original siding and trim intact, although white is not a color that would have been used in 1873.

G48 6 Bigelow Street 1872
Asbestos siding works surprisingly well on this house, almost giving the effect of scored flush boarding (as on 8 Bigelow next door, built the same year). The paired porch columns with their ornate capitals are an elegant decorative touch. An equally fine porch once adorned 5 Bigelow Street, further down the street on the other side, but a recent remodeling removed it. In sight is the rear of City Hall, where Tour H (Central Square) begins.

Tour H Central Square

Central Square proper lies at the intersection of Massachusetts Avenue and Prospect Street, where there is a subway stop. Extending east and west along Massachusetts Avenue are sections of commercial strip development that are also generally considered part of Central Square; to the north and south are residential streets that are part of the Dana Hill and Cambridgeport districts. At the western end of the Central Square commercial strip, apartment houses and civic buildings predominate; the eastern end, beyond Lafayette Square, merges into a semi-industrial zone that continues along Massachusetts Avenue to M.I.T. and along Main Street to Kendall Square. Connecting with the Dana Hill tour, Tour H begins at City Hall (Massachusetts Avenue and Bigelow Street).

The route heads generally east, with detours both north and south into residential (or formerly residential) neighborhoods. The tour ends at Technology Square, a new office-and-research complex a few blocks from Kendall Square, where the M.I.T. tour begins and where transportation is available. The architecture to be seen is enormously varied, from early 19th-century houses and stores through a century and a half of civic, religious, commercial, industrial, and residential structures. As recent developments such as Central Plaza (H17) indicate, the boom is only beginning in Central Square.

H1

H1 City Hall 1888
LONGFELLOW, ALDEN & HARLOW

Cambridge's most important civic building was donated, along with the Public Library (G9) and Manual Training School, by Frederick H. Rindge, who specified the moralistic texts above the front entrance. Longfellow, Alden & Harlow's competition-winning design is a symmetrical version of Richardsonian Romanesque, built in two colors of stone and imposingly sited above the street. The second-floor City Council Chamber, two stories high, is a handsome interior space; it is usually open during city office hours.

H2 872 Massachusetts Avenue 1964
J. TIMOTHY ANDERSON

872 is the newest and largest apartment building along the Massachusetts Avenue commercial-residential strip. Apartments begin at the third story, with offices and parking below. Projecting concrete balconies are the building's most distinctive feature.

H3 840–864 Massachusetts Avenue 1925
G. U. JACOBS

Modern Manor represents an earlier attempt than 872 Massachusetts Avenue to shield living units from traffic noise and congestion. Apartments are arranged around a sunken central courtyard, with shops along the street front. All the apartment buildings in the vicinity occupy the sites of 19th-century mansions; only the smaller houses survive, since they are built on smaller lots and are more adaptable to modern uses.

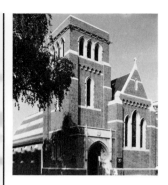

H4 St. Peter's Episcopal Church 1864–1867; 1932

WOODCOCK & MEACHAM, A. R. ESTY;
ALLEN & COLLENS

Underneath this conservative brick facade lies a wooden Gothic Revival church of the 1860's. Polychrome roof slates attest to the building's 19th-century core. Originally board-and-battened, the church was altered to its present form by Allen & Collens in 1932. The original congregation still occupies St. Peter's, despite the neighborhood's change from single-family to multiunit dwellings.

H5 Y.M.C.A. 1896; 1910

HARTWELL, RICHARDSON & DRIVER;
NEWHALL & BLEVINS

Built in two stages (the part on the corner first), the Y was an imposing structure with a monumental terra-cotta entrance portal and a tile-roofed loggia along the front of the top story. Removal of these distinguishing features has left a rather barren brick block, relieved only by a few traces of Newhall & Blevins ornament, such as leaded-glass windows and terra-cotta roundels.

H6 Post Office 1932

CHARLES R. GRECO

The granite Central Square Post Office is a good example of "P.W.A. Modern," still with original fixtures and fittings. Ornament of a streamlined classical nature is an important design element; so are formality and solidity, aspects also of the previous century's Classical Revival. The symmetrical entrance facade appropriately faces City Hall, although a utilitarian truck loading dock in the rear gives a better idea of what really goes on in a post office.

H7

H7 763 Massachusetts Avenue 1888
JOHN A. HASTY

This retail, office, and residential structure was built for the Cambridge Mutual Fire Insurance Company at the same time as City Hall, in a comparable (if fussier) Richardsonian style. The polychrome stonework would benefit from a cleaning such as City Hall was given in 1967. A cupolaed tower emphasizes the building's important corner location, a challenge not taken up by the Brusch Medical Center (1950, E. P. Graham) on the other side of City Hall (corner of Bigelow Street).

H8 St. Mary's Syrian Church 1822

Built in Lafayette Square for a Universalist congregation, this much-altered structure was moved to 8 Inman Street at the time City Hall was being built. The church suffers from the absence of its steeple, which dated from an 1858 remodeling by Thomas Silloway.

H9 12 Inman Street 1966
J. TIMOTHY ANDERSON

Inman House, a seven-story apartment building, replaces the last remaining single-family residence in the block between Massachusetts Avenue and Austin Street. The building's name recalls an important pre-Revolutionary mansion that once stood across the street. (A granite tablet in front of 15 Inman marks the site.)

H10 17 Inman Street 1871

This mansard cottage gains in stature because of its high embankment and steep, cupola-crowned roof. Elaborate wooden ornament adds to the Victorian effect.

H11 19–21½ Inman Street 1874–1876

Good neighbors to 17 Inman are these three brick row houses built a few years later. The elaborate ornament includes stone rope moldings, incised window lintels, paired brackets, and foliate column capitals. Unusual for Cambridge is the survival of all three original doors. Cambridge row houses were generally built three or four at a time by a single owner, then sold off individually (or kept in one ownership, as here). Cambridge was too suburban for entire blocks to develop with such rows, as in Boston's Beacon Hill, South End, and Back Bay. . .

H12 22–24 Inman Street 1856
MOSES AND JEDEDIAH RICKER, BUILDERS

A double Italian villa with original massing and fenestration but inappropriate modern siding. The same builders were responsible for a nearly identical house at 15–17 Lee Street at the same time. The tour now reverses direction and proceeds left on Austin Street.

H13

H13 Y.W.C.A. Addition 1964
ANDERSON, BECKWITH & HAIBLE

This dormitory wing of the Y.W.C.A. (H14) is sympathetic to the original building in color, in surface material, and even in its overhanging eaves, while remaining a clear statement of the architecture of its time.

H14 Y.W.C.A. 1910
NEWHALL & BLEVINS

Built the same year that Newhall & Blevins were expanding the Y.M.C.A. (H5), the Y.W. is fortunate in still having its open roof loggia, the most notable feature of this U-shaped, villa-like, stuccoed building. A wing was added and the entrance changed in 1953 by architects Anderson & Beckwith; the same firm added the swimming pool in 1961. Two decades earlier they had designed M.I.T.'s pool (I37).

H15 130 Austin Street 1960
SERT, JACKSON & GOURLEY

The architects of Harvard's Holyoke Center were responsible for this headquarters building for the New England Gas and Electric Association. A number of Holyoke Center's features—notably translucent wall panels between vertical slats—were first tried out here.
The tour proceeds left at the corner of Prospect Street.

H16 Prospect Congregational Church 1851

ALEXANDER R. ESTY

This fine Romanesque Revival church of the pre-Richardsonian era has round arches, corbel tables, and similar stylistic features applied to a traditional New England church type. The brick was originally stuccoed and scored in imitation of ashlar masonry. The original congregation still uses the building, which has a rear vestry added in the same style by architect Thomas Silloway in 1879. At this point, retrace your steps down Prospect Street past Austin Street to Central Square proper.

H17 Central Plaza 1967

EDUARDO CATALANO & ASSOCIATES

Newest addition to Central Square is this thirteen-story office tower. A low wing of shops and offices along Prospect Street connects with the NEGEA building (H15); a garden and parking lot along Temple Street complete the block-sized project. The tower and its two neighbors (H18–19) are best seen from across Massachusetts Avenue by the Central Square Building (H20).

H18 Cambridgeport Savings Bank Building 1904

W. E. CHAMBERLIN & C. H. BLACKALL

Monumentally classical, this building still serves the bank for which it was built. Like a number of buildings in the Central Square vicinity, it takes good advantage of its corner location. Temple Street's name comes from a Masonic temple that formerly stood on this corner.

H19

H19 719 Massachusetts Avenue 1912

SHEPLEY, RUTAN & COOLIDGE

Inspired by Renaissance palaces and loggias, this handsomely proportioned structure was built as the administrative headquarters of the Cambridge Electric Light Company. The Gas and Light Companies now have their offices and showroom in Central Plaza.

H20 Central Square Building 1926

BLACKALL, CLAPP & WHITTEMORE

Cambridge's first—and for years, only—skyscraper is ornamented with cast-stone panels in the manner of tall office structures of the twenties. Its structural skeleton can be determined from the regular bay spacing.

H21 First Baptist Church 1881

HARTWELL & RICHARDSON

The roots of this church go back to 1816, when the city's first Baptist meeting house was built on this prominent site. A successor church of 1866 burned in 1881; this building utilizes the old foundations but otherwise is a new creation. Handsome brickwork and a tall copper-crested steeple are distinguishing features of Hartwell & Richardson's design. Current development plans call for the demolition of this important Central Square landmark; the land is exceedingly valuable, and the church no longer needs such extensive facilities.

H22 Municipal Building 1933

PUTNAM & COX

Reminiscent of Parisian architecture in the way it turns the corner, the Municipal Building has "modernistic" iron grillework like its contemporary, the Post Office (H6). The Cambridge Police Department has its headquarters here.

H23 26–32 River Street 1860

This row is noteworthy for its staggered siting—each house projecting in front of the next—and for its elaborate (though crumbling) brownstone trim. Ornament on the first-floor window and door lintels includes hands holding wreaths and garlands. A comparable row, conventionally sited, is in East Cambridge (83–95 Third Street, J10).

H24 45–49 River Street 1874

An early (for Cambridge) tenement block, with a store at the corner and flats on each floor. This type of low-cost urban dwelling was to supercede row housing. When the type became more respectable (not until the nineties in Cambridge), the apartment house as we know it today evolved. The detailing of this building—even of the store front—is remarkably original; usually such structures get covered with artificial siding. Proceed down noisy River Street, against traffic coming north from the Massachusetts Turnpike. Where Pleasant Street crosses River, turn left on Cottage Street (unmarked by a street sign).

H25

H25 50 Cottage Street 1844
50 Cottage Street is the smallest and least altered of a series of Greek Revival cottages that gave this street its name. Although remodeled since the photograph above was taken, the house maintains its original massing and most of its detail and trim.

H26 40 Cottage Street 1839
This cottage is the central one of three that have Doric-columned front porches and overhanging gables. This house and number 44 have been changed through the addition of shed dormers and new siding, obscuring much original trim; number 36 has had a story added. Nonetheless, all three houses preserve enough of their original charm to make Cottage Street one of the most attractive streets in Cambridgeport.

H27 30–34 Cottage Street 1881
This block of three row houses is later in date than the adjoining cottages. The original clapboards and ornamental brackets survive, a pleasant contrast to the many remodeled houses in the vicinity.

H28 Pilgrim Congregational Church 1871

JAMES H. SPARROW AND THOMAS W. SILLOWAY

Applied wooden ornament, coarse in nature, is the most interesting feature of this unfortunately resided church, the exterior of which was designed by architect Thomas Silloway. The plan (sanctuary over ground-floor parish hall) was by local builder James Sparrow. A tall spire once topped the corner tower.

H29 39–41 Magazine Street 1856

Despite asbestos siding, this center-gable double house holds its own on its nicely landscaped corner lot. Magazine Street was—and is—Cambridgeport's finest residential street, with a number of mansions (mostly gone) as well as more modest dwellings such as the double house next door at 45–47.

H30 55 Magazine Street 1902

H. D. JOLL

Magazine Street has its share of apartment buildings, although not so many as Harvard Street (Tour G) or Linnaean Street (Tour F). The Kensington is one of the earliest, built on the "decker" or "French flats" principle, with apartments of many rooms each. Here, the presence of wings in back (compare 1010 Massachusetts Avenue, G23) allowed four flats per floor originally—now further subdivided. On the opposite corner of Upton Street is Arden Court, a slightly later (1909) court-oriented stuccoed building by Newhall & Blevins.

H31

H31 Grace Methodist Church 1886
F. E. KIDDER
Quite a contrast to Pilgrim Congregational Church (H28) is the admirable state of preservation of this church:
doors, windows, spire, and exterior
shingling are all intact. Here the ornament is integrated into the total architectural scheme rather than being
superficially applied. Beyond the
church lies Dana Square, one of
several Cambridgeport open spaces
planned by the Dana family, important
early landowners here as well as on
Dana Hill.

H32 50–52 Magazine Street 1852
This double Greek Revival-going-
Italianate house has different siding on
its two halves, but use of the same
colors—buff trimmed with brown—
makes the difference seem less obvious. Fragments of a cast-iron fence
survive along Magazine Street; elaborate iron balconies also survive above
projecting bays on the street facades.

H33 48 Magazine Street 1875
This robustly detailed mansard single
house is in commendably original
condition in spite of conversion to
multifamily use. It stands taller than
the three-decker next door, built in
1903 (C. H. Bartlett, architect).

H34 34 Magazine Street 1855
JAMES H. SPARROW, HOUSEWRIGHT

Looking like a 20th-century suburban Colonial because of its replacement porch columns and maple-leaf shutters, this modestly bracketed center-hall house actually dates from the mid-19th century. Beyond, 30–32 Magazine Street (of the same period and style as 39–41 Magazine, H29) is a prime example of the ungainliness inflicted by insensitively applied aluminum siding.

H35 16–18 William Street 1828
STEPHEN D. BROWN, HOUSEWRIGHT

This finely preserved double house is a good example of vernacular Federal architecture, comparable to the Nichols house in Harvard Square (C5).

H36 27–29 William Street 1838
The stylistic phase following that at 16–18 William Street can be seen here and in a similar double Greek Revival house at 23–25 William, on the opposite corner of Magazine. Columns are more properly Greek, gables are treated as pediments, and all trim is bolder and heavier.

H37

H37 13–21 Magazine Street 1871
Allston Terrace, a brick mansard row, was named for artist Washington Allston, whose studio stood on this site and whose house was nearby at 172–174 Auburn Street. At the latter address, a brick house built in 1855 replaces the dwelling Allston inhabited. Allston was married to Martha Remington Dana, whose family owned considerable land in Cambridgeport.

H38 Greek Orthodox Church 1935
EDWARD B. STRATTON
Following a traditional Orthodox plan, domed and centralized, this multi-colored granite structure replaces an earlier (1917) church belonging to the same congregation. The attached Educational Center was designed in 1964 by Edward J. Tedesco Associates. On the other side of Franklin Street, at 12 Magazine Street, an 1856 house by James Sparrow survives in pristine condition amid a commercial block.

H39 653–655 Massachusetts Avenue 1814
Underneath projecting storefronts, aluminum siding, and billboards is a wooden three-story house that is one of the oldest Central Square buildings. Built in 1814 by Thomas Dowse, an amateur bibliophile and art collector, it served as his home and leatherdressing shop. An orchard occupied the rest of the block through to Austin Street. Next door at 643–649 Massachusetts Avenue is an 1880 brick building that once housed the post office. In front is a new subway escalator exit, representative of design changes being made throughout the MBTA system by Cambridge Seven Associates.

H40 633 Massachusetts Avenue 1950

Neo-Georgian Woolworth's replaces an outdated (but much grander) mansard block. Another imposing mansard-roofed commercial structure formerly stood at the southeast corner of Central Square; it was cut down and refaced to create the bland two-story shop-and-office building there now.

H41 620 Massachusetts Avenue 1908

NEWHALL & BLEVINS

White terra cotta ornaments the facade of the Chronicle Building, only the ground story of which has been remodeled (and not badly, at that). Tall ogival arches subsume three stories of triple windows. Compare the Central Square Building (H20), built nearly two decades later, for a similar facade executed in cast stone rather than terra cotta.

H42 Odd Fellows Hall 1884

HARTWELL & RICHARDSON

Like other Central Square commercial buildings, Odd Fellows Hall is all facade, but it's a grand one. Round-arched and highly ornamented with molded brick, it towers above its neighbors both in height and in quality. The brickwork recalls that on the First Baptist Church (H21), a contemporary work by the same architects. Ground-story stores were part of the original scheme, although inevitably they have received new fronts; above, the facade is entirely original, complete to the raised gold lettering ending with an emphatic period.

H43

H43 452–458 Massachusetts Avenue 1806–1807

These two attached buildings are the oldest surviving commercial-residential structures in the city and among the oldest buildings in Cambridgeport. When built by the Dana family, South Row (as the block was known) extended to the corner of Brookline Street. The end buildings (452–454 and its counterpart, now demolished) had hip roofs and five-window facades along the sides; the intermediate buildings (there were two more besides 456–458) had gable roofs and Federal-style third-story windows. The two surviving buildings have had their facades stuccoed and other changes made, but the upper portions remain fairly intact.

H44 430–442 Massachusetts Avenue 1890

GEORGE FOGERTY

As a date on the brownstone pediment indicates, this monumental commercial-residential structure was built in 1890. The owner was Frank A. Kennedy, whose cracker factory (later absorbed by the National Biscuit Company) stood behind, on Green Street. Once crowned by a giant Kennedy cracker box (intimations of Pop Art), the pilastered, hip-roofed factory can be seen between the Kennedy block and 452–458 Massachusetts Avenue. The Kennedy block itself, an imposing Roman-brick structure with brownstone trim and copper bays, contains stores on the ground floor and sixteen apartments above. The storefronts date from 1940 (William L. Galvin, architect).

H45 Lafayette Square Fire Station 1893

CONDON & GRECO

Architecturally desolate at present, Lafayette Square was once quite distinguished. Through most of the 19th century a spired meeting house (now on Inman Street, H8) stood where the Shell station is; a schoolhouse formerly occupied the site of this fire station. For a later, more elaborate fire station by Charles R. Greco, see the one in Taylor Square (E48). Next door, a new Salvation Army Citadel (1968, Symmes, Maini & McKee) is replacing a terra-cotta-fronted structure of 1912.

H46 893–907 Main Street 1870

Recently remodeled below but mostly authentic above, this mansard-roofed structure was one of the city's earliest store-and-tenement blocks (compare 45–49 River Street, H24). Commercial uses were part of Main Street-Massachusetts Avenue architecture from the beginning, but earlier commercial-residential buildings followed the principle of shop below, single living unit above (as at 452–458 Massachusetts Avenue, H43), whereas here there are several floors of flats above the shops. The Kennedy block (H44) is a continuation of the latter principle, with more refined architectural definition of the components of a flat.

H47 St. Paul A.M.E. Church 1883
THOMAS W. SILLOWAY

Thomas Silloway's lavishly decorated wooden churches seem to have suffered more than most the ravages of artificial siding—compare his Pilgrim Congregational Church on Magazine Street (H28). Despite imitation brick and a truncated steeple, however, this gabled, corner-towered church still has its original massing and trim, plus a contemporary minister's house next door at 39 Austin Street. The tour proceeds right on Austin Street, then left on School Street to the corner of Pine.

H48 1 Pine Street 1840

The way in which this well-preserved Greek Revival single house and its corner garden embellish the neighborhood is a good argument against aluminum siding and parking lots, two current local threats. Nearby at 16–18 Pine Street, an 1854 double house has been rescued from derelict condition through efforts of neighborhood groups, the Cambridge Corporation, and Polaroid; furthermore, a tot lot next door has been created where a parking lot had been planned. Developments such as these bode well for the future of the neighborhood. At the corner of Eaton Street, turn right toward the rear of the Margaret Fuller House (H49).

H49

H49 Margaret Fuller House 1807

When we imagine the paved playground to the rear as a garden and the basement-level recreation hall to the side as a two-story ell, this Federal-style house at 71 Cherry Street begins to come to life. Birthplace in 1810 of Transcendentalist Margaret Fuller, the house devolved later in the 19th century into tenements and has been a settlement house since 1902. It deserves full restoration to make it a focus of neighborhood pride and attention. The tour proceeds south on Cherry Street to School Street, then left to the corner of Windsor, where the Boardman School (H50) is located.

H50 Boardman School 1868
H. B. DENNISON

No longer used for its original purpose, this is Cambridge's oldest surviving public school building. Built of brick on a plan of four corner classrooms per floor, it reminds us of how simple educational methods and educational architecture used to be. This is the second school building on the site; the lot was donated in 1802 by Andrew Bordman, early Cambridgeport landowner, whose name (spelled slightly differently) the building bears.

H51 New Towne Court 1936
HENRY C. ROBBINS ET AL.

New Towne Court was Cambridge's first public housing project. Later additions such as chain-link fences, drying yards, acres of asphalt, and an administration and recreation building blocking the axial entrance should not be allowed to detract from the merits of the original scheme, which provided light, air, and sanitary housing where very little had existed before. A subsequent project north of Harvard Street (Washington Elms, 1941, Perry Shaw & Hepburn) provided for more people on a smaller site.

H52 770 Main Street 1922

This reinforced concrete factory with brick infilling and metal sash is now—like many of its neighbors—occupied by the Polaroid Corporation. A similar building, entirely of concrete and still with wooden six-over-six sash on the front, stands on Main Street at the corner of Osborn (730 Main, 1919).

H53 708 Main Street 1882

A plaque on the corner marks this location as the site in 1876 of one end of the first long-distance telephone conversation. The present building was constructed six years later. It is a well-preserved three-story brick factory with granite sills, wooden-sash, segmental-arched lintels, and projecting brick cornice. Original doors (no longer used) survive at one of the Main Street entrances. A long, two-story ell with simpler detailing extends along Osborn Street, another along the left side of the lot.

H54 Technology Square 1961–1965

CABOT, CABOT & FORBES ASSOCIATES;
EDUARDO CATALANO; PIETRO BELLUSCHI

This new office and research center stands on land cleared of tenements and obsolete factories through urban renewal. The two identical flanking structures (545 and 575), with their filmstrip-like windows, were built in 1961 and 1963 to designs by Cabot, Cabot & Forbes Associates. The rear building (565) is a Catalano design of 1965. Belluschi and Catalano collaborated on Polaroid's headquarters (549), also a 1965 design. Oriented more toward M.I.T. than toward Central Square, Technology Square is just a few blocks down Main Street from Kendall Square, where transportation is available and where Tour I (M.I.T.) begins.

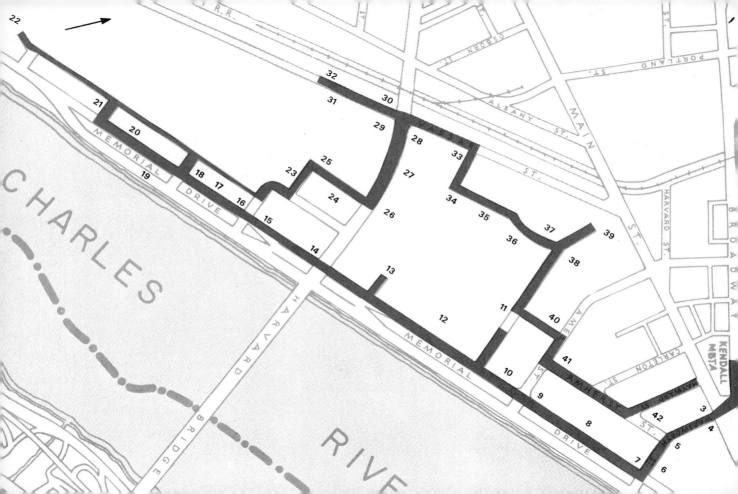

Tour I M.I.T.

The M.I.T. tour covers a part of the city that was hardly built upon before the present century, because the land was largely under water until the Charles River Embankment was created in the 1880's and 1890's. Kendall Square received a few buildings (long gone) after construction in 1793 of the West Boston Bridge (where the Longfellow Bridge is today); canals were built in hopes of creating a commercial port— thus the name Cambridgeport, now generally associated with the area around Central Square. This early development was short-lived because the Embargo of 1807 and the War of 1812 brought shipping activities to a halt. The Kendall Square district developed industrially rather than commercially, and its character is again changing—in the direction of scien-tific research—now that NASA (I1) has come. The Harvard Bridge (along Massachusetts Avenue) was completed in 1890; the filled land around it was meant to be a residential district (see Ashdown House, I14), but the coming of M.I.T. in 1913–1916 drastically altered this plan. Most of Tour I consists of M.I.T. buildings, including some of the city's best modern architecture. With one exception (an 1895 warehouse, I30), all buildings on the tour are 20th-century; unlike all the other tours, there are no private houses. Tour I begins and ends at Kendall Square, a convenient transportation point.

I1   NASA Electronics Research Center 1968

EDWARD DURRELL STONE; THE ARCHITECTS COLLABORATIVE

Built on reclaimed industrial land and on a filled-in portion of the early 19th-century Broad Canal, NASA has sparked extensive redevelopment in this formerly grim industrial district. The focus of activity is shifting, as this project indicates, from manufacturing to research. Edward Stone designed the NASA tower and the low building along Broadway (to the left in the model above). TAC designed the buildings behind (to the right in the model).

I2   Cambridge Gateway   1968

EMERY ROTH & SONS

This office and research complex for the Badger Company includes parking and shopping facilities. The name Cambridge Gateway is appropriate in that the Longfellow Bridge route has been an important approach to the city since construction of the West Boston Bridge in 1793. One of the good features of Kendall Square redevelopment is that new buildings such as this are not being built at the expense of significant earlier ones.

I3   Kendall Square Building   1917; 1925

WILLIAM MOWLL; FRANKLIN E. LELAND

Built in two stages by two different architects, this brick structure makes an attempt at monumentality in its central clock tower and applied classical trim. Long the principal landmark of Kendall Square, the building is now over-shadowed by its high-rise neighbors. Although there was some commercial activity along Main Street during the 19th century, Kendall Square did not come into its own as a business center for the surrounding industrial community until after the opening of the Cambridge subway in 1912. A power plant for the subway occupies the angled intersection of Main Street and Broadway.

14 Eastgate 1965
EDUARDO CATALANO

Twenty-nine stories of apartments for married M.I.T. students and faculty, Eastgate is sited at an angle to Kendall Square but parallel to Memorial Drive. To be joined in time by a companion tower, the building is part of a complex designed by M.I.T. Professor Eduardo Catalano. Eastgate is currently the city's tallest building in number of stories; the top floor is devoted to lounges, meeting rooms, and laundry facilities, taking advantage of the extensive view.

15 Grover M. Hermann Building 1964
EDUARDO CATALANO

The Hermann Building's poured concrete construction, projecting upper stories, regular fenestration, and battlement-like slits are characteristic Catalano design elements. Housing the Dewey Library and academic offices, the building opens on a plaza built above an M.I.T. parking facility; an upper-level bridge connects to the Sloan Building (16). Down Amherst Street, to the right, can be seen the rear of 100 Memorial Drive (18); strip windows indicate the location of corridors every three stories.

16 50 Memorial Drive 1938
DONALD DesGRANGES

M.I.T.'s Sloan Building was built as the corporate headquarters of Lever Brothers, a firm that has roots in 19th-century Cambridgeport, where soap-making was a leading industry. Formality and symmetry take precedence in the design over such 1930's details as rounded corners at the entrance. The lobby is decorated with murals of Boston and Cambridge scenes by Francis Scott Bradford. The Sloan Building accommodates M.I.T.'s School of Management and Faculty Club.

17 70 Memorial Drive 1946
PERRY, SHAW & HEPBURN

Much more "modern" than the former Lever headquarters is this laboratory-and-office building for the National Research Corporation. White glazed brick and horizontal bands of windows are combined with a centralized, almost classical entrance treatment. Counteracting the effect of rigidity are off-center steps and a canopy, the latter designed to follow the curve of a driveway that was never built.

18 100 Memorial Drive 1949
BROWN, De MARS, KENNEDY, KOCH, RAPSON

A team of architects was responsible for this pioneering Cambridge apartment house, designed to take maximum advantage of the riverfront site. A skip-stop elevator system and corridors at the rear of the building permit nearly every apartment (most with balconies) to benefit from the view. Even the entrance is in back, on Amherst Street, permitting a sunken garden instead of driveways and parking on the river side. The original building on this site was a stucco-covered 1908 Exposition Building that foretold M.I.T.'s domed classical style.

19 President's House 1916
WELLES BOSWORTH

Appropriately formal for its function as the official residence of M.I.T.'s president, this austere limestone villa—now happily vine covered—was part of Bosworth's original scheme for the Institute. Its corner site is walled off on two sides by M.I.T.'s first dormitories, now Senior House, built at the same time as the President's House and also designed by Bosworth. The architect envisioned the eastern part of the campus as the residential and social center. His plan was followed until the thirties; after the war, the West Campus (117 etc.) began to be developed with dormitories and recreational facilities.

I10 Walker Memorial 1916
WELLES BOSWORTH

Also part of the initial M.I.T. scheme was this gymnasium and dining hall, named for Francis Amasa Walker, president of the Institute from 1881 to 1897. Severely classical like all of early M.I.T., the building fittingly evokes images of Roman baths and gymnasia. By the river, on axis with Walker Memorial's portico and steps, is a sailing pavilion (1936, Harry J. Carlson).

I11 Green Building 1964
I. M. PEI

Contrasting with the horizontally organized Institute buildings of half a century earlier, this earth-sciences tower was M.I.T.'s first high-rise structure. Despite its vertical orientation, its bay system and concrete color help it to blend with its earlier neighbors. The Green Building stands alone as the focus of McDermott Court, the left wall of which is a new Chemistry Building also designed by I. M. Pei. A stabile by Alexander Calder—commissioned for the spot—stands where McDermott Court opens to the river. The tour will return to this point later, on the way back to Kendall Square.

I12 Hayden Library 1949
VOORHEES, WALKER, FOLEY & SMITH;
ANDERSON & BECKWITH

A postwar compromise between M.I.T.'s traditional architecture and full-fledged modern, Hayden suffers by comparison with contemporary Institute buildings such as Baker House (I17). Perhaps its neighbors, the Maclaurin Buildings (I13) and Walker Memorial, were too much of a restraining influence. A comparable situation occurred at Harvard at the same time—see Lamont Library (A63). Besides housing the main M.I.T. library, Hayden contains an art gallery with shows open to the public.

I13

I13 Maclaurin Buildings 1913
WELLES BOSWORTH

Named for Richard C. Maclaurin, the M.I.T. president under whom the Institute's move from Boston to Cambridge was accomplished, the Great Court is Cambridge's best example of monumental Beaux Arts classicism. Symmetrical wings and subsidiary courts focus on a broad Ionic portico and a low Roman dome, under which the original M.I.T. library was placed. Construction is of reinforced concrete clad in limestone; the vertical window units are of steel. Continuous internal corridors connect all sections of the building, and a minimum of bearing walls permits flexible interior arrangements.

I14 Ashdown House 1900
H. B. BALL

Built as Riverbank Court, a luxurious apartment hotel, M.I.T.'s Ashdown House (a residence for graduate students) recalls the period before the Institute came to Cambridge, when this filled land by the river was projected as a fashionable residential area. The building's neo-Tudor style, with turrets, parapets, and bay windows, provoked a host of lesser imitators in Cambridge apartment houses of the succeeding two decades (compare 10 Dana Street, G30). Ashdown House is H-shaped in plan, with a smaller court at the rear of the building. Harvard Bridge, which connects the Back Bay of Boston with Cambridge, was completed in 1890 and rebuilt in 1926.

I15 McCormick Hall 1962–1967
ANDERSON, BECKWITH & HAIBLE

Twin residential towers connected by lower reception and dining wings constitute this living facility for women students of M.I.T. Limestone cladding echoes earlier Institute buildings rather than McCormick's immediate neighbors.

I16 350 Memorial Drive 1901

C. H. BARTLETT

This brick-and-limestone turn-of-the-century structure (pre-M.I.T.) was built as a private hospital, serving as such—under various ownerships—until 1968, when the Institute took it over.

I17 Baker House 1947

ALVAR AALTO; PERRY, SHAW & HEPBURN

One of M.I.T.'s—and Cambridge's—most famous buildings. Baker House follows an undulating plan to provide a river view for as many of its rooms as possible. A double-tiered, limestone-clad, hard-edged lounge structure contrasts with the textured brick main mass at one of the concave parts of the curve. Stairways cling to the rear of the structure, where the entrance is.

I18 372 Memorial Drive 1917

One of several M.I.T. fraternity houses along the riverfront, Theta Delta Chi is faced with Roman brick trimmed with limestone on a granite base. On the opposite corner of Endicott Street, a more conventional red-brick Georgian Revival building houses Phi Beta Epsilon (400 Memorial Drive, 1916, George F. Shepard). Attached to the latter and numbered 403 Memorial Drive is Delta Kappa Epsilon (1925, Felix A. Burton).

I19 Pierce Boathouse 1965

ANDERSON, BECKWITH & HAIBLE

Built on piles in the Charles River, this wooden boathouse has docks on one side and an open second-story deck overlooking the Boston skyline.

I20 Burton House 1926–1928

SILVERMAN, BROWN & HEENAN

These conventional 1920's apartment buildings have flat facades, constricted courtyards, and a modest amount of cast-stone trim—quite a contrast to earlier and more lavish Ashdown House (I14). Built privately as the Riverside apartments, the buildings were acquired by M.I.T. in 1950. Attached to Burton House at 428 Memorial Drive is a red-brick neo-Georgian fraternity house, the Number Six Club (1913, Bigelow & Wadsworth).

I21 MacGregor House 1968

PIETRO BELLUSCHI; THE ARCHITECTS COLLABORATIVE

M.I.T.'s newest dormitory, part of a larger projected complex, consists of an irregularly shaped tower and a U-shaped four-story structure forming an open court. In contrast to earlier riverfront buildings, the court opens not toward the river but toward the playing fields behind. Turn in from Memorial Drive here, and look left to the next entry, which is a rather long walk away.

122 Westgate 1962

HUGH STUBBINS & ASSOCIATES

This married-student housing facility stands at the opposite end of M.I.T. from Catalano's Eastgate (14). Built of reinforced concrete infilled with brick, the project consists of a sixteen-story tower and four lower buildings surrounding a courtyard-playground. Walk back now toward the main campus, keeping the playing fields on your left. At the rear of Burton House is a handsome raised steel-and-glass dining room added in 1960 by William H. Brown and Eduardo Catalano. Note the clinging staircases on the rear of Aalto's Baker House.

123 Kresge Auditorium 1953

EERO SAARINEN

Kresge consists of an auditorium atop a small theater, both under a shell roof that is supported at only three points, allowing the exterior to be enclosed by thin-mullioned curtains of glass. Kresge rises out of a circular brick terrace across an open lawn from the M.I.T. chapel (124), also designed by Eero Saarinen, who provided a master plan for the area. Saarinen's plan was not fully executed, but the chapel and auditorium were sited as he intended.

124 M.I.T. Chapel 1954

EERO SAARINEN

Contrasting with the openness of Kresge, the chapel presents a closed face to the world. A brick cylinder set in a moat, with varying arches at the base, the building is entered from behind through an unobtrusive corridor and is topped by a sculptural bell tower by Theodore Roszak. Inside, light reflected from the moat's water casts a flickering glow on the undulating brick walls. A delicate bronze-toned screen by Harry Bertoia hangs behind the white marble altar block. Interior arrangements are flexible to accommodate various types of services. An organ is located in a balcony above the entrance.

125

125 Julius Adams Stratton Building 1963
EDUARDO CATALANO

Forming a backdrop to the West Plaza, the Stratton Building (M.I.T.'s Student Center) contains dining rooms, meeting rooms, a branch of the Harvard Cooperative Society, and other facilities. Hovering planes of concrete project out over the lower stories; monumental staircases divide the building in half, both inside and out. Vertical slits in parapets add a medieval touch—not inappropriate so close to neo-Tudor Ashdown House (114), DuPont Gymnasium (129), and the Metropolitan Storage Warehouse (130) —while the concrete color is keyed to the limestone of the Rogers Building across Massachusetts Avenue.

126 Rogers Building 1937
WELLES BOSWORTH; HARRY J. CARLSON

A Massachusetts Avenue entrance to the Institute had been intended from the start but was not designed in this form until M.I.T.'s acquisition of West Campus lands in the 1930's. Following the stylistic lead of the Maclaurin Buildings (113), to which it connects, the Rogers Building has an Ionic colonnade capped by a low dome (the coffered ceiling of which is open to view in the balconied lobby). Used by the School of Architecture and Planning, the Rogers Building connects on the end toward the river with the Pratt School of Naval Architecture, an earlier (1919) Bosworth design.

127 Center for Advanced Engineering Studies 1966
SKIDMORE, OWINGS & MERRILL (CHICAGO)

This new Skidmore, Owings & Merrill building continues its older neighbors' lime stone cladding and integrated fenestration (here in horizontal rather than vertical bands), creating a feeling that is not unclassical but avoiding overt stylistic references. The Guggenheim Aeronautical Laboratory (1927, Harry J. Carlson) adjoins on the north.

128 Metals Processing Laboratory 1950

PERRY, SHAW, HEPBURN & DEAN

This Perry, Shaw building represents an earlier break than SOM's with the limestone classical tradition for M.I.T.'s public facades. Actually, buff-colored brick had been used from the start for the rear of Institute buildings; here the material is used on all four sides of this dignified, if unexciting, structure.

129 Du Pont Center Gymnasium 1902

HARTWELL, RICHARDSON & DRIVER

Built by the city as an armory, this crenellated fortress-like structure was acquired by M.I.T. in 1957. Anderson & Beckwith's brick-fronted addition to the east was built in 1958.

130 Metropolitan Storage Warehouse 1895

PEABODY & STEARNS

This warehouse was the first large building on filled land between the railroad (which parallels Vassar Street) and the Harvard Bridge. It established the castellated style that dominated the district until the arrival of M.I.T. Ashdown House (1900, 114) and the gymnasium (1902, 129) are the two most important nearby structures influenced stylistically by the warehouse, the rear half of which was added by Peabody & Stearns in 1911.

130

131 Rockwell Cage 1947
ANDERSON & BECKWITH

Anderson & Beckwith were the pioneers of modern architecture at M.I.T. Glass-walled, clear-span Rockwell Cage, for example, is attached to their Briggs Field House of 1939. Also of that year is their Alumni Pool (137). Through unassuming athletic facilities such as these, new stylistic currents infiltrated the Institute's classical bastions.

132 West Garage 1963
MARVIN E. GOODY; CARLTON N. GOFF

One of three sizable parking facilities built by M.I.T. in the present decade, this reinforced concrete structure contains five levels of parking. On the street side, an expressive glass-and-concrete staircase defines the connection between the entrance and ramp area and the main garage space. Another stair at the far corner (out of sight) includes a bridge across the railroad tracks that parallel Vassar Street. Turn around here, and walk back across Massachusetts Avenue on Vassar Street. Across from the Institute's power plant begins a series of Skidmore, Owings & Merrill buildings.

133 Center for Space Research 1965
SKIDMORE, OWINGS & MERRILL (CHICAGO)

Window units here are recessed well behind the reinforced concrete skeleton. Except for the ground story, no limestone cladding is used (unlike SOM's Center for Advanced Engineering Studies, 127, or Vannevar Bush Building, 134), but narrow wood strips were used in the formwork for the more exposed structural members. Follow the roadway under the building.

134 Vannevar Bush Building 1963

SKIDMORE, OWINGS & MERRILL (CHICAGO)

The Main Building's dome hovers somewhat eerily above this new structure, the earliest of the SOM group. The detailing resembles that on the Center for Space Research, except that there are twice as many vertical structural members, and they are clad in limestone. To the right is visible the rear of the Center for Advanced Engineering Studies (also limestone clad). The tour proceeds to the left, under a bridge that was designed to coordinate with the Compton Laboratories (135) beyond.

135 Karl T. Compton Laboratories 1955

SKIDMORE, OWINGS & MERRILL (NEW YORK)

SOM's New York office is here represented by a laboratory building reminiscent of the firm's Lever House in New York (1952), to which Lever Brothers moved its corporate headquarters from 50 Memorial Drive (16). Aluminum-and-glass curtain walls outside the structural skeleton create quite a different effect from the forceful external grids of concrete now so much in fashion (133).

136 Dorrance Laboratories 1950

ANDERSON, BECKWITH & HAIBLE

The Compton Laboratories are attached by a glass-enclosed bridge to this earlier curtain-wall laboratory, M.I.T.'s first building to exceed five stories in height. The same architects designed the attached Whittaker Building in the same style in 1963. Dorrance and Whittaker together wall off the north side of McDermott Court, where I. M. Pei's Green Building (111) is located.

I37 Alumni Swimming Pool 1939
ANDERSON & BECKWITH
Anderson & Beckwith's Alumni Pool introduced the International Style to M.I.T. Among the building's noteworthy features are its off-center, corner-windowed entrance, its sharp-edged cubistic masses, and its south facing window wall opening on an enclosed garden. The Whittaker Building now shades the pool's sun court.

I38 ONR Generator 1948
ANDERSON & BECKWITH
This post-World War II design by Anderson & Beckwith continues the principles of the International Style. The building's expressive form results from its function of housing a Van de Graaff generator.

I39 East Garage 1960
MARVIN E. GOODY; CARLETON N. GOFF
This steel-framed, cagelike, continous-ramp garage with helical exit ramp was the first of M.I.T.'s three new parking facilities (compare the West Garage, I32). The most striking of the three, not on the tour route, is Perry, Dean, Hepburn & Stewart's reinforced-concrete Albany Street garage (1965). The tour now proceeds back into McDermott Court, past the Green Building (I11), and left at the Calder sculpture.

I40 East Campus Dormitories 1923–1930
WELLES BOSWORTH; COOLIDGE & CARLSON

Built during the twenties as part of Welles Bosworth's scheme to have residential and social quarters on the eastern part of the campus, these two long dormitory rows adjoin the rear of Walker Memorial (I10) and are close to the original Institute dormitories (now Senior House) across Ames Street by the President's House (I9). Subsequent M.I.T. dormitories, beginning with Baker House (I17), were built on the West Campus.

I41 79 Amherst Street 1912
MONKS & JOHNSON

This 1912 reinforced-concrete factory building has detail of the sort Frank Lloyd Wright sometimes used. Like many factories in the vicinity, it has been converted for use by M.I.T.—in this case, very handsomely (1962, Marvin E. Goody). Continue along Amherst Street past the rear of 100 Memorial Drive (I8) toward the Hermann Building (I5).

I42 1–23 Amherst Street 1930
DENSMORE, LeCLEAR & ROBBINS

Another factory building taken over by M.I.T., although not yet converted, this building is brick-faced and has vertical piers, cast-stone trim, and metal sash. A block up either Hayward Street or Wadsworth Street is Kendall Square, where the tour began and where transportation is available to other parts of Cambridge or to Boston.

Tour J East Cambridge

East Cambridge was one of the city's three principal centers during the 19th century—the others being Old Cambridge (Harvard Square) and Cambridgeport (Central Square). The district was laid out on a grid pattern of streets in 1810 after access from Boston had been provided by the Canal or Craigie's Bridge (where the Charles River Dam and the MBTA viaduct are now). Developer of the area was Andrew Craigie; his associates in the Lechmere Point Corporation included Christopher Gore and Harrison Gray Otis, whose names are recalled in Gore and Otis Streets. In 1813 the Lechmere Point Corporation arranged to bring the Middlesex County courts and jail to the district by providing free land and buildings; the county seat has been in East Cambridge ever since. Part of the original courthouse still survives (J8), although it is soon to be replaced. Manufacturing came early.to East Cambridge, notably in the buildings of the New England Glass Company (long gone); industry now completely surrounds the residential district, which occupies the slopes of a hill formerly topped by a Revolutionary fort (now the site of the Putnam School, J33). The houses of East Cambridge are representative of modest vernacular architecture from the period 1820–1870, their context if not their physical condition relatively unspoiled. The tour begins and ends at the Lechmere MBTA station, where public transportation is available.

J1

J1 108 Cambridge Street 1866

East Cambridge from the start was an industrial as well as a residential district, with industry located on the periphery of the residential area. The earliest factories have disappeared, but this brick structure (originally a furniture factory) survives from the third quarter of the 19th century. Enlarged several times since then, it now accommodates the Deran Confectionery Company (whence emanates from time to time a delicious smell of chocolate). A less pleasantly odiferous 19th-century East Cambridge industry, now gone, was that of pork rendering and packing, the subject of many neighborhood complaints.

J2 Registry of Deeds and Probate Court 1896

OLIN W. CUTTER

The Registry of Deeds and Probate Court is the most monumental of Middlesex County's 19th-century structures, all of which are scheduled to be replaced. Four giant brick-columned porticoes are the building's most distinctive feature. Steep flights of stairs ascend on the Cambridge and Otis Street facades; inside, a tall, balconied central space (now cluttered by conference-room partitions on the main floor) gives access to Registry facilities on the Third Street side and to Probate facilities on the Second Street side. Handsome iron lanterns adorn the Second Street basement entrance.

J3 County Bank 1965

SYMMES, MAINI & McKEE

Spurred in part by new courthouse construction, private redevelopment is occurring in East Cambridge. This branch office of the County Bank will be joined in time by a new head-quarters building for the Middlesex County National Bank, to be located diagonally across the intersection of Cambridge and Second Streets. The County Bank's low structure is in scale with East Cambridge domestic architecture, but its construction involved the demolition of several good 19th-century brick buildings. It represents the "new" East Cambridge at the expense of the old; ideally, both should be able to exist together.

J4 30–34 Second Street 1836–1839
These three brick row houses look
somewhat forlorn now that their
original number has been reduced by
two to make way for bank parking.
Still, they recall the early domestic
character of East Cambridge, where
modest single, double, and row houses
were the rule for the first three-quarters
of the 19th century. Planar wall surfaces and brick dentil cornices are
characteristic of the 1830's in East
Cambridge (compare a slightly earlier
and more elegant row at 262–266
Cambridge Street, J39).

J5 36–46 Second Street 1842
Frame construction was more common than brick in East Cambridge, as
in the city as a whole. Unfortunately,
modern siding more often than not
obscures the original appearance of
the district's wooden buildings. Here,
a different kind or color of siding is
used on each of the six houses in the
row. Underneath can be seen traces of
a heavy Greek Revival entablature;
projecting entrance porches (some
with replacement columns) are the
most obvious surviving stylistic
features.

J6 2–28 Otis Street 1869–1871
This four-story brick structure with
regular bay treatment and segmental-
arch window caps is typical of
industrial architecture of the last third
of the 19th century. Built as a factory
for furniture and woodwork, it is still
used for its original purpose, although
not by the original firm. When the
factory was built, tidal waters of the
Charles came nearly to First Street (at
the end of the block).

J7

J7 Clerk of Courts Building 1889
ROBERT P. WAIT & OLIN W. CUTTER

Built for the Probate Court, this structure was subsequently given over to the Clerk of Courts. Stylistically the building echoes Ammi Young's 1848 courthouse next door (J8), particularly in its round-arched windows, pilasters, and projecting pedimented central section, but the trim is brownstone instead of granite or cast iron, and the scale is more monumental. In the 18th century, the river's waters reached this point, as evidenced by the fact that British troops landed here en route to Lexington and Concord in April 1775 (see the granite tablet along Second Street).

J8 Superior Court Building 1848
AMMI B. YOUNG

This 1848 structure by Ammi Young incorporates in its center section the original East Cambridge courthouse, built in 1814 to plans by Charles Bulfinch. Now hemmed in by later construction, the building originally faced an open courthouse square. The present pressed-brick exterior dates from an 1898 remodeling; the 1848 finish was stucco scored in imitation of ashlar masonry. Inside, the ground story has brick vaulting and heavy iron doors designed for fireproof storage of records; the two upstairs courtrooms still have original furniture. All will be destroyed when construction of the new courthouse complex proceeds into this block.

J9 55–61 Otis Street 1851

This row of four Greek Revival town-houses is one of the finest in the city. Granite is used for foundations and steps, unornamented brownstone for sills and lintels; an elaborate cast-iron balcony extends across the second-floor front, where the principal parlors were located. Built as single-family residences, all four houses in the row have been converted to flats, as have most houses in East Cambridge. Originally the cornice was continuous; the top stories of the middle two buildings were added around the turn of the century to make room for fourth-floor flats.

J10 83–95 Third Street 1860
Representing a later style of row-house construction than 55–61 Otis Street, these seven attached houses have high stoops, mansard roofs, and no rear ells. They are more akin to houses in Boston's South End than to those of Beacon Hill, although lacking the South End's characteristic bow fronts. Brownstone has taken the place of granite for foundation and steps, and lintels are highly ornamented rather than plain. Together with Holy Cross Church (J11), the row makes a handsome blockfront across from the old courthouse.

J11 Holy Cross Polish Church 1827
Built for a Unitarian congregation, this Federal-style meeting house is the third oldest church building in the city, after Christ Church (E3) and St. Mary's Syrian Church (H8). Although it has lost the cupola that surmounted its tower, it is otherwise in much its original condition. The broad entrance tower and shallow recessed window arches are characteristic features. The stained glass and much of the interior furniture date from the later 19th century, when an Episcopal mission owned the building.

J12 New Superior Court Building 1968
EDWARD J. TEDESCO ASSOCIATES
New facilities for the county courts have been needed for some time; the only direction to go was up. The first stage of this three-block project is a tower (East Cambridge's first skyscraper) on the site of the former county jail. Subsequent stages will extend the complex to Cambridge Street.

J13

J13 Third District Court 1931
CHARLES R. GRECO
Construction of this court building, which infringes upon East Cambridge's best residential area, necessitated the demolition of a number of 19th-century houses. At least the new court facilities will leave the residential streets alone, although the old county buildings will have to go. Greco, a versatile local architect, here designed in a conventional Georgian Revival idiom; at the same time he was capable of more stylish efforts, such as the stripped-down classicism of the Central Square Post Office (H6).

J14 59 Thorndike Street 1827
Built at the same time as the church to which it is attached, this house has always been privately owned, never serving as parish house or rectory. Since no additional row houses were built to the west, the house has always stood tall and somewhat aloof. Stylistically, it is of a type that continued for twenty years or more—compare 63 Sciarappa Street (J35), another solitary row house, built in 1846. The large projecting roof dormer is not original, but the entrance door and iron balcony probably are. An ample side yard provides welcome breathing space in this densely settled neighborhood.

J15 69 Thorndike Street 1845
A fine example of East Cambridge's detached wooden houses is this side-hall Greek Revival model, which preserves its original siding. Flush boarding is used under the porch and in the pediment; clapboards are used elsewhere. Two-over-two sash replace six-over-six, and the entrance door and frame are new; otherwise, the house retains an authentic appearance, complete to pedimented gable, wide corner pilasters, and Ionic porch columns.

J16 71–73 Thorndike Street 1844–1847
This double house of the same period as its next-door neighbor (J15) suffers from the addition of inappropriate siding and sash, but it retains its original massing and front porch. A curious feature is the suggestion of a pediment in the central lift of the porch entablature.

J17 74 Thorndike Street 1843
Unusual for East Cambridge is this T-shaped Greek Revival house with two-story openwork corner pillars. Also unusual for East Cambridge is the building's derelict condition.

J18 80 Sciarappa Street 1846
With its pedimented facade facing Thorndike Street and its entrance facing Sciarappa (formerly Fourth) Street, this house utilizes every inch of its corner lot. The first-story windows have pedimented lintels, and the iron-work balcony follows a simple rectilinear design. The double entrance is unusual in that the left half was the "front door" and the right half the "back door"—rarely placed so close to each other.

J19

J19 85 Thorndike Street 1822
Diagonally across from 80 Sciarappa Street stands this 1822 center-hall house, which later in the 19th century was embellished with brackets and a projecting shingled entrance bay. Its back-from-the-street setting gives an almost country feeling compared to its neighbors on the other three corners.

J20 84–94 Thorndike Street 1867
FRANCIS H. STICKNEY AND BENJAMIN F. DAVIES, BUILDERS
This brick mansard row is conservative for its date by comparison with 83–95 Third Street (J10). The two houses nearest the corner have been thrown together into one, with an unfortunate change in first-floor fenestration.

J21 96 Thorndike Street 1826
Obviously earlier than its neighbors, this house has a brick front, an arched entrance recess, and a wooden fanlight in the gable. Fireplaces in the front rooms are located between the two left-hand facade windows, but the chimney changes direction to emerge from the gable in a centralized position.

J22 116 Thorndike Street 1865
Refreshingly authentic in exterior appearance, this side-hall house with bracketed entrance bay and round-headed gable window puts its newly renovated neighbor at number 118 to shame. Only the fine iron fence at the corner of Fifth Street remains to indicate the latter's former character.

J23 146 Thorndike Street 1829
This simple house and its twin at the back of the lot exemplify an early East Cambridge type—the worker's cottage. Built end-to-street with the entrance at the side of the lot, such cottages were an alternative to row housing. A variety of mid-19th-century gable-ended houses can be seen looking back from here toward Fifth Street.

J24 156 Thorndike Street 1855
Variety in East Cambridge comes not only from housing types but also from siting. Here a corner is left open for a garden, overlooked from the side piazza of this bracketed house. Across Thorndike Street, quite a different effect is created by the tall masonry hulk of Sacred Heart Rectory (1885).

J25

J25 East Cambridge Branch Library 1938

McLAUGHLIN & BURR

Like most East Cambridge buildings, this civic facility is hardly an architectural monument, but it is simple enough to wear well. The basement of this branch library contains the city's 19th-century tax records, which were used to date most of the buildings in this guide. A school formerly stood here.

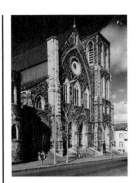

J26 Sacred Heart Church 1874

P. W. FORD

Victorian Gothic in blue slate trimmed with granite, Sacred Heart is East Cambridge's most imposing church. The steeple once soared to a height of 170 feet. The marble altar inside was imported from England in 1882, the year the building was completed. The altar survived a 1963 fire intact, but the rest of the interior required substantial redecoration.

J27 140 Otis Street 1895

JOHN MULDOON

Occupying the site of an earlier building, this Colonial Revival house—now a funeral home—is unique in East Cambridge. Most of the district's late 19th-century construction took the form of tenements on the backs of lots, increasing the density without contributing much in the way of architectural effect. Having a sizable, stylish house across from Sacred Heart Church was —and is—quite an asset, although artificial siding has taken its toll.

J28 134 Otis Street 1868
This bracketed side-hall single house
remains in exemplary condition. Two-
over-two sash here were original
rather than being later replacements as
at 69 and 71–73 Thorndike Street
(J15–16), built two decades earlier.
The plan is still the side-hall type, but
instead of two square rooms off the
stair hall there is one long parlor.
Dining room and kitchen are in the ell.

J29 122–124 Otis Street 1870
Another house in pristine condition—
this one a mansard-roofed double
house with bracketed eaves and door
canopies. A similar house at 118 Otis
Street has been over-renovated.

J30 103–105 Otis Street 1843
This Greek Revival double house is
comparable to 71–73 Thorndike Street
(J16) but is more intact. Note that the
main body of the house is only one
room deep.

J31

J31 St. Hedwig's Polish Church 1939
F. F. McDONOUGH
This yellow-brick, cast-stone-trimmed, corbel-tabled church replaces a 19th-century wooden church (originally Universalist) that blew down in the hurricane of 1938. St. Hedwig's is a good example of institutional design that fits in well with its domestic neighbors.

J32 100 Otis Street 1848
Three stories high and built of brick, 100 Otis Street is one of the most substantial free-standing houses in East Cambridge. The first-story brownstone lintels are slightly pedimented, one of the few concessions to Greek Revival "style," so much more blatantly proclaimed on wooden houses such as 103–105 Otis Street (J30). 100 Otis Street now serves as the rectory for St. Hedwig's Church. The brick double house next door at 102–104 Otis was also built in 1848; its entrance doors and mansard roof were added later.

J33 Putnam School 1887
JAMES FOGERTY
This three-story red-brick schoolhouse is the city's best surviving example of a fast disappearing type; perhaps it can be converted to other uses when the new Robert F. Kennedy School is completed. The Richardsonian arched entrance, brick patterns under the window arches, elaborate cornice, and gabled, dormered roof are all features of distinction. The site is an important one, too; a granite plaque near the corner notes the presence here of Revolutionary Fort Putnam, from which British troops were bombarded during the Siege of Boston, 1775–1776.

J34 80–82 Otis Street 1861
An appropriately imposing brick double house for this high point of East Cambridge land. Conservative for 1861 in having a pitched roof, the house is up-to-date in having ornamental brownstone window lintels and projecting bays. The tot lot across Otis Street was formerly occupied by several buildings, including a Gothic Revival church built in 1842 (St. John's, the first Catholic church in Cambridge).

J35 63 Sciarappa Street 1846
Now connected with Guardian Hospital, this brick row house was originally free-standing. Stylistically it resembles 55–61 Otis Street (J9), although it is a story lower and lacks ornamental ironwork. Still, it is grander than the adjoining row of four very narrow wooden houses at 53–59 Sciarappa Street (1883), recently re-shingled in a way that obscures their original wooden trim. A single-family house formerly stood on the hospital's corner lot.

J36 337–343 Cambridge Street 1883
Cambridge Street has had commercial architecture combined with residential since the district's earliest days. This brick block—a replacement for earlier buildings on the same site—has stores on the ground story (considerably remodeled) and tenements above, a standard pattern in the later 19th century. Earlier commercial-residential buildings generally had a single living unit above each store, rather than flats, as here.

J37

J37 St. Francis of Assisi Church 1837
Built as a Baptist meeting house in 1837, this church was remodeled first in 1868 (when the bracketed pediment took its present form) and again in 1932 (when the campanile was added by the Italian Catholics). Next door at 307–311 Cambridge Street is an 1898 store-and-tenement block with considerably less character than 337–343 (J36) or than the adjoining store-and-hall block at 303–305 (1876).

J38 East Cambridge Savings Bank 1931
THOMAS M. JAMES
This handsome granite structure is lavishly adorned with exterior ornament by sculptor Paul Fjelde and painted ceiling decorations by Alfred Rasmussen. Representing a sizable financial investment for East Cambridge during the Depression, it replaced a smaller turn-of-the-century bank on the same site. Its quality, style, and condition are such that it deserves a longer life than its predecessor.

J39 262–266 Cambridge Street 1830
Built a century earlier than the East Cambridge Savings Bank, these two row houses represent another era in the district's history. Except for doorway changes at 262 and replacement sash, the houses are in substantially original condition. Arched door openings are a mark of the Federal style; so are flat, unornamented facades and unobtrusive dormers (compare Greek Revival row houses such as 63 Sciarappa Street, J35). When the houses were built, there was a Methodist church at the corner and a parsonage between; another church was subsequently built, only to be demolished for the present parking lot.

J40 Middlesex County National Bank 1917

THOMAS M. JAMES

This bank building by the architect of the East Cambridge Savings Bank (J38) is designed in the early 20th-century classical style (compare the Cambridgeport Savings Bank Building, H18). Built of cast stone as opposed to the granite of East Cambridge Savings, and less distinctively ornamented, the building will not be particularly missed when the Middlesex Bank's new complex reaches this corner of the block. Two doors down at 215–217 Cambridge Street, a pavilioned, mansarded Odd Fellows Hall (1862) is also slated to be demolished; its loss is more to be regretted.

J41 47–51 Gore Street ca. 1820

Although substantially altered over the years, this row of four houses represents the initial East Cambridge style — vernacular Federal, as at 262–266 Cambridge Street (J39), only simpler. Put up by the Lechmere Point Corporation, the row is designed as a unified architectural composition. The two end buildings (25 Third Street and 51 Gore Street) have entrances in the middle of the side facades; the center buildings (47 and 49 Gore Street) follow the standard row-house plan. The original roof slope survives on the right-hand two buildings. Across Third Street is a double brick tenement house with a mansard roof and a later corner store (41–43 Gore Street, 1868). The fire station on the opposite corner is an 1894 design, Georgian Revival in style.

J42 26 Gore Street ca. 1836

At the corner of Gore and Second Streets stands this isolated survival from early East Cambridge. Built as a store building, it has a large hall (entered from stairs at 3 Second Street) on the third floor. Its roof is a combination of hip (on the Second Street side) and gable (on the Third Street side, where it could have connected with another building but never did). A block further down Gore Street is the Lechmere MBTA station, where the tour began.

CITY OF CAMBRIDGE

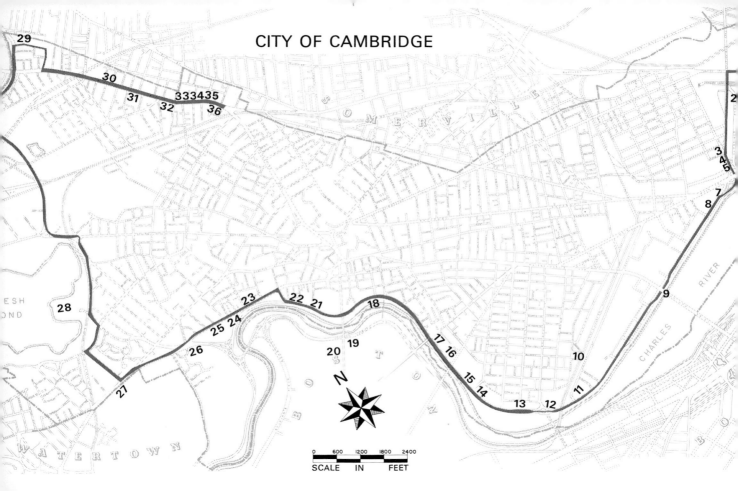

SCALE IN FEET

0 600 1200 1800 2400

Other Points of Interest

Several parts of the city—notably the riverfront and North Cambridge—have buildings that are worthy of inclusion in a Guide to Cambridge Architecture but that are too limited in number or too spread out to make walking tours feasible. This final section of the Guide covers a number of these points of interest, beginning at the Charles River Dam, continuing along the city's extensive river frontage, and concluding along upper Massachusetts Avenue between Alewife Brook Parkway and Porter Square.

The riverfront is one of the city's greatest environmental assets. Though its landscaped banks look natural, they are entirely man made; a century ago the Charles River was an irregular tidal stream bordered by marshes and mud flats. During the 1880's and 1890's an embankment was built along most of Cambridge's river frontage, with a landscaped parkway (the forerunner of today's Memorial Drive) along the new shoreline. Sponsored first by the Charles River Embankment Company and then by the Cambridge Park Department, the project was assured success when the Charles River Dam was built in the years 1903–1910, stabilizing the Basin's water level. For the first time in the city's history, buildings could be designed to face the river rather than having to turn their backs on it because of ugliness and stench. The points of interest on the riverfront portion of this tour are therefore all of the 20th century, with the exception of Fort Washington (O10), built during the Revolution but now entirely cut off from the river, and the Riverside Press (O16), a pre-embankment industry on the site of a former city almshouse.

North Cambridge, with upper Massachusetts Avenue as its spine, had a few houses and farms in the 17th and 18th centuries but grew to its present form in the latter half of the 19th century and the early years of the 20th. Nearly all traces of earlier settlement, including several sites associated with the Revolution, have been obliterated or obscured, but the residential streets off Massachusetts Avenue have a pleasant if unassuming character. Selected North Cambridge buildings (O29–36) are included here for their architectural interest and because of their landmark status in the surrounding community.

01

01 Museum of Science 1951–

AMES, CHILD, GRAVES; PERRY, SHAW,
HEPBURN & DEAN; E. VERNER JOHNSON,
ROBERT N. HOTVEDT & ASSOCIATES

Half in Boston and half in Cambridge, the Museum of Science stands in Science Park, an extension of the Charles River Dam. After acquiring the site in 1949, the museum built the present east wing in 1951 (Ames, Child, Graves), the central Countway Building in 1960 (Perry, Shaw, Hepburn & Dean), and a parking garage on the Cambridge side in 1967 (E. Verner Johnson & Associates). The newest building, begun in 1968, is a sizable west wing linking the Countway Building and the garage. E. Verner Johnson, Robert N. Hotvedt & Associates are the architects of the new wing. The museum originated as the Boston Society of Natural History, founded in 1830.

02 Charter House Motor Hotel 1961

CURTIS & DAVIS

The Charter House fronts on Cambridge Parkway, a post-World War II development on filled land along the river. Most of the buildings on Cambridge Parkway are research laboratories built between 1946 and 1951; several are now occupied by M.I.T. The Charter House differs from its neighbors in height, function, and date. Its eight stories of guest rooms take advantage of the river view; beneath their vertical block extends a glass-fronted story of dining and function rooms above a street-level parking area.

03 Cuneo Press 1895

LOCKWOOD, GREENE & CO.

Built for the Athenaeum Press, the production branch of Ginn & Company, the Cuneo Press building at 215 First Street was one of the earliest and largest industrial plants along Cambridge's reclaimed riverfront. Structurally, it represents a continuation of 19th-century mill construction techniques. Built of brick with brownstone lintels and a copper cornice, the building originally had a terra-cotta statue of Athena crowning its central pediment.

O4 Carter's Ink Company 1909
DENSMORE & LE CLEAR

More innovative structurally than the Cuneo Press building, the Carter's Ink building at 239 First Street is built entirely of reinforced concrete—from its basic structure to its modest facade decoration. It was one of the first reinforced concrete factories in the city and one of the few to use the material throughout; most of its successors infilled the concrete frame with brick. Still occupied by the company that built it, the Carter's Ink building is a landmark on the Longfellow Bridge approach to the city—largely because of its huge, brightly lighted rooftop sign.

O5 Cambridge Electric Light Company 1947
GILBERT ASSOCIATES, INC.

This electric power station at 265 First Street is another riverfront landmark. Although the plant's streamlined, slick-surfaced style is a far cry from the arcaded, turn-of-the-century Western Avenue power station (O17), both buildings serve the same purpose —generating electricity for Cambridge use. Alongside the building lies the Broad Canal, a survival from the early days of Cambridgeport. Until recently, coal barges used the canal to deliver fuel to industries such as Boston Woven Hose and Rubber Company; now the drawbridges are no longer raised, and the canal is being filled bit by bit.

O6 Longfellow Bridge 1900
EDMUND M. WHEELWRIGHT, CONSULTING ARCHITECT; WILLIAM JACKSON, CHIEF ENGINEER

The Longfellow Bridge occupies the site of the West Boston Bridge, the 1793 span that provided the first direct link between Boston and the eastern part of Cambridge. Originally called the Cambridge Bridge, the Longfellow Bridge was designed to accommodate rapid transit tracks, although work did not start on the Cambridge subway until 1909. Constructed of granite over a concrete core, with steel arches, the Longfellow Bridge is the most ornate as well as the oldest of the existing bridges to Cambridge. Its four central pavilions have earned it the nickname of "Pepper Pot" or "Salt and Pepper" Bridge.

07

07 Electronics Corporation of America 1920–1927
Built as a warehouse and service build-
ing for Filene's Department Store,
One Memorial Drive has anchored the
corner of Main Street and Memorial
Drive since the 1920's. Remodeled in
1956 by architect William H. Brown,
the building now serves the Electronics
Corporation of America. This shift in
use is typical of the changing character of nearby Kendall Square, where
the NASA Electronics Research Center
(I1) is being built.

08 Arthur D. Little, Inc. 1917
KILHAM & HOPKINS
Although Arthur D. Little's headquarters are now in Acorn Park, a post-
World War II industrial and research
complex in West Cambridge, the company still occupies this laboratory and
office building at 30 Memorial Drive,
built for it in 1917. Next door at 38·
Memorial Drive are the Cabot Corporation's research laboratories (1951,
E. T. Steffian and J. G. Kuhn, a rebuilding of a 1925 office building by
Harold Field Kellogg).

09 M.I.T. Riverfront
The Massachusetts Institute of Technology owns and occupies most of the
riverfront between Wadsworth and
Amesbury Streets, a distance of over a
mile. Buildings along this stretch of the
river are identified individually on the
M.I.T. walking tour (I6–I21). M.I.T.
and Harvard (O18) began developing
their riverfronts about the same time
(1913–1916); today the buildings of
these two institutions—in both cases
a combination of low-rise and high-
rise—provide an imposing introduction to Cambridge from the Boston
side of the Charles River.

O10 Fort Washington 1775

Cut off from the river by warehouses and railroad tracks stands the city's only surviving Revolutionary fortification. One of a series of half-moon batteries built by order of General Washington to protect Cambridge from attack from the river, Fort Washington survives only because it became a city park before the surrounding area began to develop industrially. The Dana family deeded it to the city in 1857, at which time an ornamental granite-and-iron fence was built. Fort Washington cannot be seen from the river, but persevering drivers can find it on Waverly Street amid trucking-company trailers.

O11 Jordan Marsh Warehouse 1913
MONKS & JOHNSON

This brick-veneered, reinforced concrete warehouse was originally a factory for the Gray & Davis Company. Jordan Marsh took it over in 1929, after rival Filene's had established a service building down the river (O7). A similar but later building adjoins at 600 Memorial Drive; now owned by M.I.T., it was built in 1926 as a factory for the Johnson-Appleby Company.

O12 640 Memorial Drive 1913
JOHN GRAHAM

Polaroid Corporation now occupies this large structure, originally a factory and warehouse for the Ford Motor Company. Brick and terra cotta cover the principal facades, although the back walls are of steel and painted glass. Crossing the river at this point is the Boston University (originally Cottage Farm) Bridge, which consists of two separate spans—one for the railroad, one for automobiles. Designed by Desmond & Lord, it was built in the 1920's by the Metropolitan District Commission, as were the next two up-river bridges at River Street and Western Avenue.

O13

O13 Morse School 1955
CARL KOCH & ASSOCIATES
Replacing a conventional three-story brick schoolhouse nearby, Morse School is a sprawling one-story complex with a maximum of indoor-outdoor access, sunlight (gained in interior corridors through skylights), and bright colors—a deliberately warm and open educational environment. On the river side of Memorial Drive lies Magazine Beach, former site of a state powder magazine, now the location of a Metropolitan District Commission swimming pool (the Charles itself no longer being fit for swimming). An antipollution facility under construction here may help clean up the river.

O14 Fenway Cambridge Motor Hotel 1966
SALSBERG & LE BLANC
The city's newest motor hotel follows the trend established by the Charter House (O2) in being located in a non-residential district along the river. Ease of access by automobile (in this case, from the Cambridge exit of the Massachusetts Turnpike) appears to have been a more important consideration than closeness to business centers, entertainment, or public transportation. Two hundred guest bedrooms fill the upper floors of this fifteen-story building; dining and function rooms occupy a lower wing toward Memorial Drive, with a swimming pool on the fifth-floor roof. A separate garage structure is attached at the rear.

O15 780 Memorial Drive 1937
COOLIDGE, SHEPLEY, BULFINCH & ABBOTT
Built for BB Chemical (whose name used to be displayed in large stylized letters at the top of the central tower), this clean-lined industrial building is now occupied by Polaroid Corporation. It is the earliest and best of the city's 1930's-modern structures (such as 70 Memorial Drive, I7) characterized by sharp edges, horizontal strip windows (often, as here, continuing around corners), and rigidly symmetrical facades. Glazed brick and glass block are other typical features.

O16 Riverside Press

This industrial complex encompasses a former city almshouse, built in 1837 and converted for book manufacturing by Little, Brown in 1851. Named the Riverside Press because of its location, it was acquired by Henry O. Houghton in 1867 and is still owned by Houghton Mifflin. Hardly anything is left of the almshouse structure (it survives at the core of the central, towered building), but there is a succession of later 19th-century and 20th-century industrial buildings. Unlike the other manufacturing complexes along the Charles, this one predated the embankment and thus does not present a coherent riverfront facade.

O17 Cambridge Electric Light Company 1901

SHEAFF & JAASTAD

Large arched window openings and tall brick chimneys give a monumental appearance to this power station at Memorial Drive and Western Avenue. Detracting from the original design are new window sash and a raised brick parapet that replaces an open iron balustrade. Harvard gets the steam to heat its buildings from this power plant.

O18 Harvard Riverfront

Covered in detail on Walking Tour B, the Harvard riverfront from Peabody Terrace (B27) to Eliot House (B22) is one of the city's most outstanding sights. The Harvard buildings along Memorial Drive, besides being individually of high-caliber design, together possess sufficient mass and density to form a proper backdrop to the sycamore-lined roadway. The fact that this stretch of riverbank is actively used for recreational purposes adds to the interest of the scene.

O19 Harvard Business School 1924
McKIM, MEAD & WHITE

Located in the Allston section of Boston but oriented toward the Harvard side of the river, the Business School took form in the 1920's as the result of an architectural competition won by McKim, Mead & White. The neo-Georgian style they employed has been followed by other Business School architects nearly to the present, maintaining the consistency of the original scheme if not producing any monuments of contemporary design.

O20 Harvard Stadium 1902
GEORGE B. deGERSDORFF; CHARLES F. McKIM

Advanced for its day in being constructed entirely out of reinforced concrete, the stadium preceded even Cambridge factories (such as Carter's Ink Company, O4) in the extent of its use of this material. It dominates Harvard's athletic facilities on the Boston side of the river, approached by way of the Larz Anderson Bridge (1912, Wheelwright, Haven & Hoyt). On diagonally opposite sides of the bridge are two boathouses by Peabody & Stearns—the Newell Boat House (1899) on the Boston side and the Weld Boat House (1906) on the Cambridge side.

O21 Conventual Church of St. Mary and St. John 1936
CRAM & FERGUSON

Adjoining the MBTA car yards (future site of the Kennedy Library) are this Episcopal church and its related monastery buildings serving the Society of St. John the Evangelist. Church specialists Cram & Ferguson were the architects, here working in an archaeologically correct Burgundian Romanesque style. The plan of the church emphasizes the choir area because of the building's function as a conventual rather than a parish church. A partially completed cloister garden provides a pleasant setting on the east side.

022 992–993 Memorial Drive 1914
W. L. MOWLL

This six-story, court-oriented apartment house (originally known as Strathcona-on-the-Charles) was the first of four such buildings constructed on this stretch of riverfront in the years before and after World War I. The building's form and style are familiar from such earlier structures as Riverbank Court (now Ashdown House, I14) and Burton Halls (G30). The plan of many-bayed Strathcona follows the curving frontage of the irregular site. Before the river parkway was built, a gas works stood here; in the 17th century a windmill was located at the end of Ash Street, then known as Windmill Lane.

023 221 Mt. Auburn Street 1962
HARRIS & FREEMAN

It took an urban renewal project to clear the way for this apartment building, appropriately called Riverview. The apartments open toward the river through a grid of concrete balconies. Parking space, screened from Mt. Auburn Street, is provided behind and under the building. A row of town houses (22–28 Bradbury Street) is also part of the Riverview project, which has spurred considerable private redevelopment in this district of modest 19th-century workers' houses.

024 1010 Memorial Drive 1963
COHEN HAFT & ASSOCIATES

A soaring vertical contrast to the horizontal of Riverview, 1010 Memorial Drive rises twenty stories above its surroundings to produce views that extend to downtown Boston and beyond. Living rooms of 1010's apartments are on the balconied river facade, which is angled to permit maximum exposure; bedrooms and services are behind. Parking is out of sight in an underground garage topped by a terraced garden. 1010 stands on the former site of Harvard's Stillman Infirmary, now part of Holyoke Center (B9).

O25

O25 Mt. Auburn Hospital 1884
WILLIAM E. CHAMBERLIN
Founded in 1883 as the Cambridge
Hospital, Mt. Auburn Hospital still
occupies its original buildings, although their use has changed and
numerous additional structures have
been built. The hospital's main entrance
is now at 280 Mt. Auburn Street, in a
1959 structure designed by Marcus &
Nocka. W. E. Chamberlin's original
grouping at 330 Mt. Auburn Street
consisted of a three-story main building and two subsidiary wings—one a
men's ward, the other a women's.
Beyond, at 360 Mt. Auburn Street, is
the Cambridge Home for Aged People
(1898, Stickney & Austin).

**O26 10 Coolidge Hill Road
1807–1809**
Coolidge Hill is a residential enclave
cut off from the rest of Cambridge by
traffic on the parkways. A few houses
(such as this one) survive from the
19th century, when most of the hill
was a Coolidge farm. Of interest nearby
are the neo-Georgian Forbes house
(1911, Joseph Everett Chandler) at 30
Gerry's Landing and two postwar
houses by Carl Koch (40 Gerry's
Landing, 1946, and 44 Gerry's Landing,
1946). A Federal house moved in from
Harvard Square is at 144 Coolidge
Hill, and the much-remodeled
Coolidge farmhouse is at 24 Coolidge
Hill Road.

O27 Mt. Auburn Cemetery 1831
Although its grounds are almost entirely in Watertown, Mt. Auburn Cemetery has traditionally been associated
with Cambridge and Boston. Inspired,
founded, and partly designed by a
Boston physician, Jacob Bigelow,
Mt. Auburn was the first garden cemetery in America, setting a much emu-
lated precedent. The Egyptian Revival
gateway, designed by Dr. Bigelow,
was built of Quincy granite in 1843,
replacing an earlier roughcast wooden
gateway of the same design. Within the
cemetery are a granite Gothic Revival
chapel, a tower at the crest of the
highest hill, and over a century of
funerary and horticultural art.

O28 Fresh Pond

Now a reservoir bordered by a municipal golf course, a park, and waterworks, Fresh Pond is the only sizable body of water within the city limits. In the 19th century Fresh Pond was an important source of ice and a popular recreation spot, the center of activities being the Fresh Pond Hotel (later removed to 234 Lake View Avenue and converted to apartments). Although the banks of Fresh Pond are protected, the environs consist of a banal series of automobile-age services—restaurants, shopping centers, car dealers, filling stations, and a drive-in movie.

O29 Immaculate Conception School 1850

LOUIS DWIGHT AND G. J. F. BRYANT

Originally the Cambridge Almshouse (replacing an earlier almshouse that became the nucleus of the Riverside Press, O16), this mid-19th-century stone structure on Matignon Road once stood alone amid the Poor Farm's fields and orchards. Designed on the institutional pattern of central block with radiating wings, the building is still intact outside, with only a few later appendages (such as a sunporch on the front wing, an extended right wing, and new stair towers). Related buildings are Immaculate Conception Church on Alewife Brook Parkway (1928–1934, John A. McPherson) and Father Matignon High School (1946, Maginnis & Walsh).

O30 2343 Massachusetts Avenue 1886

J. SEWELL & CO.

Since the 17th century, upper Massachusetts Avenue has been a thoroughfare to points north and west. Sparsely settled for the first two centuries, it began to be built up with substantial residences in the second half of the 19th century. The past fifty years have brought so much commercial development (mostly one-story stores) that only a few of the avenue's houses have survived. This one, a brick-and-shingle Queen Anne design in immaculate condition, was built for John E. Parry of the brick-making family (compare 140 Upland Road, F37).

O31

O31 St. John's Church 1904
MAGINNIS, WALSH & SULLIVAN

St. John's Church with its tall campanile is a North Cambridge example of Italian Romanesque, a popular style for early 20th-century Roman Catholic churches in Cambridge (compare St. Paul's Church, B44). Maginnis, Walsh & Kennedy, the original architects' successor firm, rebuilt St. John's after a fire in 1956. Another nearby church of note is Notre Dame de Pitié (1920) at Rindge Avenue and Middlesex Street. Built for a French-speaking congregation, Notre Dame was inspired by French Romanesque architecture rather than Italian.

O32 Cornerstone Baptist Church 1854; 1885
A. R. ESTY; VAN BRUNT & HOWE

Clearly a design of the 1880's in its detailing, this white-painted wooden church retains the basic towered form of the 1854 church at its core. A. R. Esty designed the original church, which was "Romanesque" like his Prospect Congregational Church (H16). Van Brunt & Howe brought the building to its present form, rebuilding the steeple and adding side aisles and a rear parish hall. The site of the 18th-century Watson house, now at 30 Elmwood Avenue (C53), was across on Russell Street where the Cambridge Nursing Home now stands.

O33 2067–2089 Massachusetts Avenue 1892
C. E. PARKE

A carriage factory has here become an automobile showroom—an appropriate adaptive use. Henderson Brothers, carriage manufacturers, built this five-story brick building to replace an earlier factory of theirs that had burned. The angled corner toward Porter Square (its arched window openings now hidden by a tall Salvi Ford sign) was originally topped by an open wooden tower.

O34 Fire Station 1896

AARON H. GOULD

One of the city's handsomest fire stations, this 1896 structure at 2029 Massachusetts Avenue combines Colonial Revival brickwork with a Renaissance arcade for the second-story windows. Refreshingly asymmetrical, the design has mass and dignity appropriate to a public edifice.

O35 St. James's Church 1888

HENRY M. CONGDON

This brick-trimmed stone church by a New York architect is intriguingly sited at the angled intersection of Massachusetts Avenue and Beech Street. A square crossing tower dominates the composition; other noteworthy elements are an apse at the east end and and an open belfry and rose window at the west end. The design is a late and free version of Richardsonian Romanesque; the interior is appropriately dark and heavy-timbered. The pre-Revolutionary Davenport Tavern formerly stood on this corner.

O36 North Avenue Savings Bank 1906

GAY & PROCTOR

This early 20th-century banking house and its next-door neighbor, the Masonic Temple (1910, F. B. Furbish), stand near the site of a former Cambridge landmark, Porter's Hotel, which gave its name to Porter Square and to the world-famous cut of meat, the Porterhouse steak. (Cattle yards were located in back, along the railroad tracks.) Porter's Hotel was a commercial and social center all through the 19th century; fortunately, its replacements here have more architectural interest than the used car lots, one-story stores, and other nondescript structures that the 20th century has brought to upper Massachusetts Avenue.

Illustration Credits

The following listing is by sources of photographs. Names of photographers, where known, are in parentheses.

Cambridge Historical Commission (Bertram Adams) H49, O10

Cambridge Historical Commission (Richard Cheek) A8–12, A14–18, A22, A24, A27, A29–30, A34–37, A39, A41, A43–45, A48–49, A51, A55–58, A60, A62, A64, A68, B1–14, B16–19, B21, B24–25, B29, B33–43, B45–50, B52–54, C2, C4–6, C11–12, C15, C20, C22, C24, C29–30, C33, C40–41, C48, D1–6, D8–9, D12, D17–18, D20–21, D23, D34, D36–37, D45, D55, E1–2, E4–5, E7–13, E15–16, E18–19, E22, E26, E28, E31–34, E36–37, E39, E41, E43, E46, E48, Tour F introduction, F2–13, F15–16, F18–19, F21–22, F24, F26–27, F29, F32–39, F41–44, F46–48, G1–2, G4–5, G7, G10–11, G13, G15, G18–19, G23–25, G39–41, G44, H2–6, H9, H13–15, H17–20, H23–24, H29–30, H34–35, H38–39, H41, H43–47, H50–54, I3–10, I12–16, I18–19, I22-24, I26, I29–37, I40–42, J1–2, J4, J6, J9, J16–18, J20, J22, J24, J26, J29, J32–36, O1–5, O7–9, O11–24, O26–34, O36

Cambridge Historical Commission (Elsa Craig) D48, D53, D56–57, D59, E17, E20, E23–24, E27, E29–30

Cambridge Historical Commission (Patricia Hollander) C21, C35, C42, C46–47, C49, D7, D25–26, D38, E35, E38, E45, F14, F20, F25, F40, F45

Cambridge Historical Commission (Alice Lyndon) I28, I38

Cambridge Historical Commission (Robert Nylander) A21

Cambridge Historical Commission (B. Orr) A13, A42, A47, A50, Tour B introduction, B15, B32, B44, C1, C3, C7–10, C13–14, C17–18, C23, C25–28, C31–32, C34, C36, C38–39, C43–45, C50–51, C53, D10–11, D13–14, D16, D19, D22, D24, D27–33, D35, D40, D43–44, D46–47, D49–50, D54, D60, E14, E42, E44, F23, F30–31, Tour G introduction, G3, G6, G8–9, G12, G16–17, G20–21, G26, G29–30, G32, G34–36, G38, G43, G45–46, G48, Tour H introduction, H7–8, H10, H12, H22, H25, H28, H31, H36–37, H42, J3, J5, J7, J10–11, J13–14, J19, J21, J23, J25, J27, J30–31, J37–42, O6, O25

Cambridge Historical Commission (R. B. Rettig) C16, C52, G14, G31, G33, G37, G42, G47, H11

Cambridge Historical Commission (John Terry) H33

Index

The following index is in four parts— an index of architects, builders, and artists; an index of buildings by name; an index of buildings by address; and a chronological index. All references are to *Guide* entries (A23, C40, etc.) rather than to page numbers. Introductions are not indexed because the information they contain about buildings or architects can be found in more complete form in the individual entries. The texts of the entries are indexed as well as the headings. Principal listings—those where buildings are illustrated—are printed in **boldface**.

Index of Architects, Builders, and Artists

All are architects unless otherwise noted.

Index of Buildings by Name

This index is subdivided as follows:
(A) general Cambridge buildings; (B) Harvard University buildings; (C) buildings of Harvard clubs and organizations; (D) M.I.T. buildings; (E) buildings of M.I.T. clubs and organizations; (F) Radcliffe College buildings.

Randolph Hall (Adams House),
B34, **B40**, B41
Read House (Graduate School of
Education), **C4**
Robinson Hall (Graduate School of
Design), A53, A55, **A56**, A58
Russell Hall (Adams House), B43

Sanders Theatre **A12**
Science Center, A29
Semitic Museum, A34
Sever Hall, A55, **A57**
Smith Halls (Kirkland House), **B21**
Sparks House, **A31**
Stadium, **O20**
Standish Hall (Winthrop House), B23
Stillman Infirmary, O24
Stoughton Hall, **A6**, A9, A10, E7
Straus Hall, A70, A71, B7

Tercentenary Theatre, A65
Thayer Hall, **A10**, A66

Union, A61, **A62**, E10
University Hall, **A4**, A9, A14, A35, E6
University Herbaria, A35, A37
University Museum, **A26**, A27, A35, A36

Varsity Club, A62

Wadsworth House, A60, **A72**
Warren House, A61
Weeks Bridge, **B24**
Weld Boat House, O20
Weld Hall, A68, **A69**, A70
Westmorly Court (Adams House),
B35, **B45**
Widener Library, A63–64, **A65**, A66–68
Wigglesworth Hall, A68, A71
Winthrop House, B22, **B23**

C. Harvard Clubs and Organizations
A.D. Club, **B49**
D.U. Club, **B13**, B34
Delphic Club, **B41**

Fly Club, **B37**
Fox Club, B12
Harvard Advocate, B18
Harvard Crimson, B38, **B43**
Harvard Lampoon, **B38**
Hasty Pudding Club, **B53**
Hillel House, **A44**
Institute of 1770, **B53**
Iroquois Club, **B35**, B36
Lincoln's Inn Society (Law School), **E17**
Owl Club, **B33**, B41
Phoenix-S.K. Club, **B36**
Pi Eta Club, B12
Porcellian Club, **B52**, B53, D11
Signet Society, **B14**
Spee Club, **B34**

D. M.I.T. Buildings
Alumni Swimming Pool, H14, I31, **I37**
79 Amherst Street, **I41**
Ashdown House, I14, I20, I25, I30
Baker House, E36, I12, **I17**, I22, I40

President's House, **C7**
Radcliffe Institute, **E8**
Schlesinger Library, **E8**
Whitman Hall, E36

Chronological Index
This is an index to the dates of
construction of all buildings illustrated
in the *Guide*. Just one date per building
is indexed—in each case, the earliest
date (even in the case of remodeled
or rebuilt structures). The prevalence
of 19th-century and 20th-century
architecture in Cambridge is apparent
from the distribution of dates in this
index. Following the general listing is a
breakdown of date periods by tours.

1760	B42, E3	1823	C13	1848	C12, E39, G28, G38, J8, J32
1761	C32	1825	A35	1849	F13
1762	A5, B20	1826	B18, J21	1850	C37, D12, G34, O29
1764	A3, C50	1827	C5, J11, J14	1851	D53, H16, J9
1765	C24	1828	H35	1852	C46, D52, H32
1767	C54	1829	B17, J23	1853	D41, D54, E24, G36
1772	C4	1830	J39	1854	F14, O32
1775	O10	1831	O27	1855	A51, D44, D47, G32, H34, J24
1790	E46	1833	E1	1856	A50, D49, H12, H29
1803	C33	1834	D55	1857	A67, C28, F1, G24, G33, G42
1804	A6	1836	J4, J42	1858	D38
1806	E11, H43	1837	A48, E18, J37	1859	A26, C7, D32, G35
1807	G40, H49, O26	1838	A16, A31, D4, H36	1860	B11, H23, J10
1808	C3, D1	1839	A49, B10, H26	1861	J34
1810	C43, E44	1840	G21, G26, H48	1862	A68, D31, E17, F44
1811	A9	1841	B15, E19, G27	1863	D51, F18
1812	F24	1842	E47, G14, G29, J5	1864	F45, H4
1813	A4, C16	1843	C26, J17, J30	1865	G41, J22
1814	H39	1844	C18, E23, E40, H25, J16	1866	J1
1815	F19	1845	B2, B32, D55, F47, J15	1867	G1, G18, J20
1820	B14, D55, E4, J41	1846	C23, F2, G4, G20, J18, J35	1868	D42, D60, H50, J28
1822	A61, H8, J19	1847	A13, C9	1869	A10, B50, D46, F41, J6

1870	A12, A69, E12, F16, F17, G31, G46, H46, J29	1888	A17, C45, D34, G9, G43, H1, H7, O35	1904	A58, E9, E42, E48, H18, O31
1871	A70, E32, F31, H10, H28, H37	1889	A1, A46, E25, F26, G3, G12, J7	1905	B33, D19, D50, E26
		1890	A21, A47, B52, F38, H44	1906	A19, B12, O36
1872	D24, D29, D58, E29, E33, F11, F42, G48	1891	B46, E16	1907	B51, E8
		1892	B39, C27, C35, D57, F34, O33	1908	C8, H41
1873	C44, F29, F35, G47	1893	A11, A24, C49, D11, D13, F20, G5, H45	1909	B6, B38, G30, O4
1874	C14, E30, F30, H11, H24, J26			1910	A38, D3, H14
1875	D40, E21, H33	1894	C36, C48, D35	1911	A45, A60, G37
1876	D30, F25, F43	1895	C38, C51, D10, G17, I30, J27, O34	1912	A43, F9, F21, H19, I41
1877	D22, D48, G16, G39			1913	A40, A65, B21, B23, I13, O11, O12
1878	A57, D39	1896	D16, F3, F8, H5, J2, O34		
1880	E31	1897	B8, B40, B54	1914	A32, G2, O22
1881	A15, H21, H27	1898	A8, B45, D14, E10, F4, F10, G10	1915	B36, B43, B44, C30
1882	D15, H53			1916	A44, B35, E13, I9, I10
1883	C10, C20, C47, H47, J36	1899	B37, B49, C52, G15, G23	1917	D8, I3, I18, J40, O8
1884	C39, F40, H42, O25	1900	A25, A56, A62, C42, D6, E22, I14, O6	1920	O7
1885	E27			1922	D33, E43, E45, F15, H52
1886	A37, C15, D27, F5, F6, G7, G31, O30	1901	D17, E28, E35, I16, O17	1923	B7, E15, I40
		1902	A30, B41, B48, G25, H30, I29, O20	1924	A71, B4, F33, O19
1887	B53, C21, C22, C34, F27, F28, F37, F39, G45, J33			1925	A55, H3
		1903	A52, C25, D7	1926	A42, B24, F46, H20, I20
				1927	A28, D2, D28

1928	B1, F48
1929	B19, B26, B30, B31, E6, F22
1930	A34, A36, B13, B22, G19, I42
1931	A66, B34, E7, J13, J38
1932	G8, H6
1933	G6, H22
1935	H38
1936	H51, O21
1937	D43, I26, O15
1938	A14, I6, J38
1939	C31, G11, I37, J31
1940	B47, D18
1941	A64, C11, F32
1946	I7
1947	A63, E36, I17, I31, O5
1948	I38
1949	A20, E41, I8, I12
1950	B16, D36, H40, I28, I36
1951	A29, A54, E20, O1
1953	I23
1954	D5, D56, I24
1955	D25, F7, I35, O13

1956	B3, D37
1957	A22, A41, F36
1958	B29, D26
1959	A39, B25, C6
1960	C29, E34, F12, H15, I39
1961	A59, B9, H54, O2
1962	A23, A27, G44, I15, I22, O23
1963	A33, B27, D23, I25, I32, I34, O24
1964	H2, H13, I5, I11
1965	D21, D59, E5, E37, E38, I4, I19, I33, J3
1966	C2, C41, D9, H9, I27, O14
1967	A18, B28, D45, H17
1968	D20, G13, G22, I1, I2, I21, J1 2
1969	A53

Breakdown of Date Periods by Tours

Tour	A	B	C	D	E	F	G	H	I	J	O
before 1800	5	2	10	0	4	1	0	0	0	0	1
1800–1829	5	3	6	2	3	2	1	5	0	6	1
1830–1869	11	6	9	18	9	9	19	12	0	22	3
1870–1899	14	10	19	18	11	25	17	18	1	7	6
1900–1929	19	21	4	10	13	7	4	8	11	1	12
1930–1969	18	11	6	14	8	4	7	11	30	6	9